"In this, their fourth co-authored book, the amazing trio of Lichtenberg, Lachmann, and Fosshage has creatively expanded and deepened their own already impressive contributions to the study of self-experience, exploring the process of, as they term it here, *Enlivening the Self*. Two modes of experience are scrutinized in order to conceptualise how an enlivened sense of self develops, both in infancy and then throughout life. The first mode concerns the author's more familiar territory, the individual's experience of self when he or she is attending to a specific motivational task. But even here, within their more well-travelled realm of motivational systems, the authors have something very new to offer, the elaboration of twelve research and observation-based qualities or capacities that emerge during the first year of life and that potentially serve as life-long sources of enlivenment. These twelve qualities are explored in the first essay of the volume, focused on infancy, and also in the second essay, demonstrating their clinical usefulness in the adult through two well elaborated case examples. The third essay is focussed in entirely new and original territory: the individual's sense of self when he or she is not focussed on a task, when his or her mind wanders, exploring, in this, their initial foray on the topic, how such mind wandering enlivens the self. The concept of mind wandering, as is always the case with these authors, is based in explorative research and clinical observation, and brings to our awareness an exciting and novel perspective on self-development. This is a wonderful book. I can only recommend that you see for yourself."

– **Estelle Shane**, Ph.D. is a Training and Supervising Analyst at the Institute of Contemporary Psychoanalysis in Los Angeles and a Training and Supervising Analyst at the New Center for Psychoanalysis in Los Angeles.

Enlivening the Self

In psychoanalysis, enlivenment is seen as residing in a sense of self, and this sense of self is drawn from and shaped by lived experience. *Enlivening the Self: The First Year, Clinical Enrichment, and the Wandering Mind* describes the vitalizing and enrichment of self-experience throughout the life cycle and shows how active experience draws on many fundamental functional capacities, and these capacities come together in support of systems of motivation; that is, organized dynamic grouping of affects, intentions, and goals.

The book is divided into three essays:

Infancy – **Joseph D. Lichtenberg** presents extensive reviews of observation and research on the first year of life. Based on these reviews, he delineates twelve foundational qualities and capacities of the self as a doer doing, initiating and responding, activating and taking in.

Exploratory therapy – **James L. Fosshage** looks where therapeutic change is entwined with development. There are many sources illustrated for enhancing the sense of self, and **Frank M. Lachmann** pays particular attention to humor and to the role that the twelve qualities and capacities play in the therapeutic process.

The wandering mind – **Frank M. Lachmann** covers the neuroscience and observation that "mind wandering" is related to the immediacy of the sense of self linking now with past and future.

Throughout the book the authors' arguments are illustrated with rich clinical vignettes and suggestions for clinical practice. This title will be a must for psychoanalysts, including trainees in psychoanalysis, psychiatry residents and candidates at psychoanalytic institutes and also graduate students in clinical and counselling psychology programs.

Joseph D. Lichtenberg, MD, is Editor-in-Chief of Psychoanalytic Inquiry, Director Emeritus of the Institute of Contemporary Psychotherapy and Psychoanalysis, past President of the International Council for Psychoanalytic Self Psychology, and a member of the Program Committee of the American Psychoanalytic Association.

Frank M. Lachmann, PhD, is a founding faculty member of the Institute for the Psychoanalytic Study of Subjectivity, Honorary Member, Vienna Circle for Self Psychology, The William A. White Institute, and the American Psychoanalytic Association, and Clinical Assistant Professor at the NYU Postdoctoral Program in Psychotherapy and Psychoanalysis.

James L. Fosshage, PhD, is Founding President, International Association for Psychoanalytic Self Psychology (IAPSP); Co-Founder, Board Director and Faculty, National Institute for the Psychotherapies; Founding Faculty, Institute for the Psychoanalytic Study of Subjectivity; Clinical Professor of Psychology, New York University Postdoctoral Program in Psychotherapy and Psychoanalysis. (His website is www.jamesfosshage.net.)

PSYCHOANALYTIC INQUIRY BOOK SERIES
JOSEPH D. LICHTENBERG
SERIES EDITOR

Like its counterpart, *Psychoanalytic Inquiry: A Topical Journal for Mental Health Professionals*, the Psychoanalytic Inquiry Book Series presents a diversity of subjects within a diversity of approaches to those subjects. Under the editorship of Joseph Lichtenberg, in collaboration with Melvin Bornstein and the editorial board of *Psychoanalytic Inquiry*, the volumes in this series strike a balance between research, theory, and clinical application. We are honored to have published the works of various innovators in psychoanalysis, such as Frank Lachmann, James Fosshage, Robert Stolorow, Donna Orange, Louis Sander, Léon Wurmser, James Grotstein, Joseph Jones, Doris Brothers, Fredric Busch, and Joseph Lichtenberg, among others.

The series includes books and monographs on mainline psychoanalytic topics, such as sexuality, narcissism, trauma, homosexuality, jealousy, envy, and varied aspects of analytic process and technique. In our efforts to broaden the field of analytic interest, the series has incorporated and embraced innovative discoveries in infant research, self psychology, intersubjectivity, motivational systems, affects as process, responses to cancer, borderline states, contextualism, postmodernism, attachment research and theory, medication, and mentalization. As further investigations in psychoanalysis come to fruition, we seek to present them in readable, easily comprehensible writing.

After 25 years, the core vision of this series remains the investigation, analysis, and discussion of developments on the cutting edge of the psychoanalytic field, inspired by a boundless spirit of inquiry.

PSYCHOANALYTIC INQUIRY BOOK SERIES
JOSEPH D. LICHTENBERG
SERIES EDITOR

Vol. 2
Psychoanalysis and Infant Research
Joseph D. Lichtenberg

Vol. 8
Psychoanalytic Treatment:
An Intersubjective Approach
Robert D. Stolorow, Bernard
Brandchaft, & George E. Atwood

Vol. 10
Psychoanalysis and Motivation
Joseph D. Lichtenberg

Vol. 12
Contexts of Being:
The Intersubjective Foundations of
Psychological Life
Robert D. Stolorow & George E.
Atwood

Vol. 13
Self and Motivational Systems:
Toward a Theory of Psychoanalytic
Technique
Joseph D. Lichtenberg, Frank M.
Lachmann, & James L. Fosshage

Vol. 14
Affects as Process:
An Inquiry into the Centrality of Affect
in Psychological Life
Joseph M. Jones

Vol. 16
The Clinical Exchange:
Techniques Derived from Self and
Motivational Systems
Joseph D. Lichtenberg, Frank M.
Lachmann, & James L. Fosshage

Vol. 17
Working Intersubjectively:
Contextualism in Psychoanalytic
Practice
Donna M. Orange, George E.
Atwood, & Robert D. Stolorow

Vol. 18
Kohut, Loewald, and the
Postmoderns:
A Comparative Study of Self and
Relationship
Judith Guss Teicholz

Vol. 19
A Spirit of Inquiry:
Communication in Psychoanalysis
Joseph D. Lichtenberg, Frank M.
Lachmann, & James L. Fosshage

Vol. 20
Craft and Spirit:
A Guide to Exploratory
Psychotherapies
Joseph D. Lichtenberg

Vol. 21
Attachment and Sexuality
Diana Diamond, Sidney J. Blatt, &
Joseph D. Lichtenberg (eds.)

Vol. 22
Psychotherapy and Medication:
The Challenge of Integration
Fredric N. Busch & Larry S. Sandberg

Vol. 23
Trauma and Human Existence:
Autobiographical, Psychoanalytic,
and Philosophical Reflections
Robert D. Stolorow

Vol. 24
Jealousy and Envy:
New Views about Two
Powerful Feelings
Léon Wurmser & Heidrun Jarass (eds.)

Vol. 25
Sensuality and Sexuality across
the Divide of Shame
Joseph D. Lichtenberg

Vol. 26
Living Systems, Evolving
Consciousness, and the Emerging
Person:
A Selection of Papers from the Life
Work of Louis Sander
Gherardo Amadei & Ilaria Bianchi (eds.)

Vol. 27
Toward a Psychology of Uncertainty:
Trauma-Centered Psychoanalysis
Doris Brothers

Vol. 28
Transforming Narcissism:
Reflections on Empathy, Humor, and
Expectations
Frank M. Lachmann

Vol. 29
Mentalization:
Theoretical Considerations, Research
Findings, and Clinical Implications
Fredric N. Busch (ed.)

Vol. 30
From Psychoanalytic Narrative to
Empirical Single Case Research:
Implications for Psychoanalytic Practice
Horst Kächele, Joseph Schachter,
Helmut Thomä, & the Ulm
Psychoanalytic Process Research
Study Group

Vol. 31
Toward an Emancipatory
Psychoanalysis:
Brandchaft's Intersubjective Vision
Bernard Brandchaft, Shelley
Doctors, & Dorienne Sorter

Vol. 32
Persons in Context:
The Challenge of Individuality in
Theory and Practice
Roger Frie & William J. Coburn (eds.)

Vol. 33
Psychoanalysis and Motivational
Systems:
A New Look
Joseph D. Lichtenberg, Frank M.
Lachmann, & James L. Fosshage

Vol. 34
Change in Psychoanalysis:
An Analyst's Reflections on the
Therapeutic Relationship
Chris Jaenicke

Vol. 35
World, Affectivity, Trauma:
Heidegger and Post-Cartesian
Psychoanalysis
Robert D. Stolorow

Vol. 36
Manual of Panic Focused
Psychodynamic Psychotherapy –
eXtended Range
Fredric N. Busch, Barbara L. Milrod,
Meriamne B. Singer, & Andrew C.
Aronson

Vol. 37
The Abyss of Madness
George E. Atwood

Vol. 38
Self Experiences in Group, Revisited:
Affective Attachments, Intersubjective
Regulations, and Human
Understanding
Irene Harwood, Walter Stone, &
Malcolm Pines (eds.)

Vol. 39
Nothing Good Is Allowed to Stand:
An Integrative View of the Negative
Therapeutic Reaction
Léon Wurmser & Heidrun Jarass (eds.)

Vol. 40
Growth and Turbulence in the
Container/Contained:
Bion's Continuing Legacy
Howard B. Levine & Lawrence J.
Brown (eds.)

Vol. 41
Metaphor and Fields:
Common Ground, Common Language,
and the Future of Psychoanalysis
S. Montana Katz (ed.)

Vol. 42
Psychoanalytic Complexity:
Clinical Attitudes for Therapeutic
Change
William J. Coburn

Vol. 43
Structures of Subjectivity:
Explorations in Psychoanalytic
Phenomenology and Contextualism,
2nd Edition
George E. Atwood & Robert D.
Stolorow

Vol. 44
The Search for a Relational Home:
An Intersubjective View of
Therapeutic Action
Chris Jaenicke

Vol. 45
Creative Analysis:
Art, Creativity and Clinical Process
George Hagman

Vol. 46
A Rumor of Empathy:
Resistance, Narrative and Recovery in
Psychoanalysis and Psychotherapy
Lou Agosta

Vol. 47
Enlivening the Self:
The First Year, Clinical Enrichment,
and the Wandering Mind
Joseph D. Lichtenberg,
James L. Fosshage, & Frank M.
Lachmann

Out of print titles in the PI series

Vol. 1
Reflections on Self Psychology
Joseph D. Lichtenberg & Samuel
Kaplan (eds.)

Vol. 3
Empathy, Volumes I & II
Joseph D. Lichtenberg, Melvin
Bornstein, & Donald Silver (eds.)

Vol. 4
Structures of Subjectivity:
Explorations in Psychoanalytic
Phenomenology
George E. Atwood & Robert D.
Stolorow

Vol. 5
Toward a Comprehensive Model for
Schizophrenic Disorders:
Psychoanalytic Essays in Memory of
Ping-Nie Pao
David B. Feinsilver

Vol. 6
The Borderline Patient:
Emerging Concepts in
Diagnosis, Psychodynamics, and
Treatment, Vol. 1
James S. Grotstein, Marion F.
Solomon, & Joan A. Lang (eds.)

Vol. 7
The Borderline Patient:
Emerging Concepts in
Diagnosis, Psychodynamics, and
Treatment, Vol. 2
James S. Grotstein, Marion F.
Solomon, & Joan A. Lang (eds.)

Vol. 9
Female Homosexuality:
Choice without Volition
Elaine V. Siegel

Vol. 11
Cancer Stories:
Creativity and Self-Repair
Esther Dreifuss-Kattan

Vol. 15
Understanding Therapeutic
Action:
Psychodynamic Concepts of Cure
Lawrence E. Lifson (ed.)

Enliveningthe Self

The First Year, Clinical Enrichment, and The Wandering Mind

Joseph D. Lichtenberg,
Frank M. Lachmann, and
James L. Fosshage

LONDON AND NEW YORK

First published 2016
by Routledge
2 Park Square, Milton Park, Abingdon, Oxon, OX14 4RN

and by Routledge
711 Third Avenue, New York, NY 10017

Routledge is an imprint of the Taylor & Francis Group, an Informa business

© 2016 Joseph D. Lichtenberg, Frank M. Lachmann and James L. Fosshage

The right of Joseph D. Lichtenberg, Frank M. Lachmann and James L. Fosshage to be identified as authors of this work has been asserted by them in accordance with sections 77 and 78 of the Copyright, Designs and Patents Act 1988.

All rights reserved. No part of this book may be reprinted or reproduced or utilised in any form or by any electronic, mechanical, or other means, now known or hereafter invented, including photocopying and recording, or in any information storage or retrieval system, without permission in writing from the publishers.

Trademark notice: Product or corporate names may be trademarks or registered trademarks, and are used only for identification and explanation without intent to infringe.

British Library Cataloguing in Publication Data
A catalogue record for this book is available from the British Library

Library of Congress Cataloging-in-Publication Data
Lichtenberg, Joseph D.
  Enlivening the self : the first year, clinical enrichment, and the wandering mind / Joseph D. Lichtenberg, Frank M. Lachmann and James L. Fosshage.
    pages cm
  1. Self psychology. 2. Developmental psychology.
3. Psychoanalysis. I. Lachmann, Frank M. II. Fosshage, James L. III. Title.
  BF697.L5195 2016
  155.2—dc23
  2015008178

ISBN: 978-1-138-80971-0 (hbk)
ISBN: 978-1-138-80972-7 (pbk)
ISBN: 978-1-315-74985-3 (ebk)

Typeset in Times
by Apex CoVantage, LLC

Contents

Acknowledgements	xiii
Preface	xv
I The First Year of Life	1
II Clinical Guidelines	71
III The Wandering Mind	99
Afterword: Toward a Metatheory – a Diagrammatic Portrayal	131
References	143
Index	149

Acknowledgements

We wish to acknowledge our gratitude to our patients, students, colleagues, and friends for all that they have taught us. We are especially grateful to the many infant researchers whose findings we have built on and to John Kerr for his editorial help. And, once again, we are indebted to Kate Hawes of Taylor & Francis for her assistance with our books.

Preface

This book is about feeling enlivened. For humans, feeling enlivened resides psychologically in a sense of self. An enlivened sense of self emerges from the lived experience of being a doer doing. The lived experience of being a doer doing, initiating and responding, draws animation from its embeddedness in the physical and physiological experience of a body and its relational connectedness to animate others and inanimate objects. An enlivened self-agency – that is, being a doer doing – involves many fundamental functional capacities including perception, cognition, memory, emotion, and recursive awareness. These foundational functional capacities come together in support of systems of motivation – that is, organized dynamic groupings of affects, intentions, and goals.

The three of us, Joe Lichtenberg, Frank Lachmann, and Jim Fosshage, have now coauthored four books in which we have stretched Kohut's conceptualization of a psychology of the self in various directions. And central to our work has been the expansion of a theory of motivation. In the present work, we have continued this expansion with special emphasis on what goes right in development, but not to the exclusion of how things can go awry.

Explicating seven motivational systems has been our major focus in our prior publications; the three essays of this book represent an important departure. For by the end of it, we will ultimately emphasize two distinct modes of experience – an individual's sense of self when focused on a specific motivational task, which has hitherto been our focus, and an individual's sense of self when his or her mind wanders, a new topic for us. In our view, each mode of experience contributes to the enlivening of the sense of self, particularly in the here and now. Beyond that, each mode also contributes to enlivening the sense of self through the repetition of patterns that support a sense of continuity throughout life. In our immediately prior book, *Psychoanalysis & Motivational Systems: A New Look* (Lichtenberg, Lachmann, & Fosshage, 2011), we applied the mathematical and philosophic concept of fractals (repetitions of patterns that demonstrate selfsameness over time and scale) to explain continuity of the sense of self, identity, personhood. Here we add mind wandering as an experience crucial to the continuity of the sense of self.

But first we must take up what we mean by enlivening the self and how this emerges in infancy. To that end, in our first essay, we review in detail the experiences and events critical for enlivened development during the first year of life. Here as in all of our writings, we review developmental research and observation, clinical experience, and the findings of neuroscience to delineate as much as possible a baseline of normal, healthy, adaptive development throughout the life cycle. From this perspective of adaptive lived experiences and shifting balances of self and interactional regulation that lead to happiness, productivity, and enhanced self-worth, we contrast psychic pathology. In each section we shift back and forth between adaptive and maladaptive lived experience, with an emphasis on the adaptive.

As is customary in our writing, we juxtapose direct observation with findings taken from the scientific literature. Our survey will be presented in terms of answering basic, experience-near questions about how and when the infant comes to experience himself or herself as a doer doing, both with self and with others. Then, drawing again on research and on our own observations, we will identify twelve qualities and capacities that emerge in the first year in conjunction with the infant's being a doer doing. The important point is that these qualities and capacities potentially constitute important sources of enlivenment for the sense of self *in all endeavors throughout life*. Depending on the person's early and later development, these qualities and capacities contribute to positive outcomes in exploratory treatments or make them more difficult. Here as elsewhere we emphasize that later developments – including treatment – can have significant effects, for good or ill, in terms of enlivening or deadening the self.

Then, in our second essay, we take the twelve qualities and capacities that can be identified in the first year of life and demonstrate in some detail their importance in exploratory treatments. The two featured treatments in our presentation are quite different from one another, yet it is possible in each to use the twelve qualities and capacities as benchmarks for illuminating specific clinical engagements. This we have done in our comments, which are interspersed with the case narratives. Similarly, the twelve qualities can also serve as a kind of template for understanding the overall progress, or lack thereof, of the treatment. Truly, it seems remarkable to us that qualities and capacities which can be clearly identified in the first year of life lend themselves so readily to understanding therapeutic process much later in life.

Even more remarkable in our view is the subject matter of our third essay: the wandering mind. In this essay, we will add to our prior accounts of unfolding motivation (Lichtenberg, Lachmann, & Fosshage, 2011) our recently acquired understanding of the significance of the *nontask focused* or wandering mind. Since our core concepts center on the wide-ranging use of agency, it may seem paradoxical that our depiction of a doer doing must now be expanded to include the process of a person responding mentally to a host of seemingly "stray" thoughts that occur when his or her mind is not otherwise engaged. Yet this is precisely what the neuroscientific literature now suggests is appropriate. It appears that those passing thoughts are not stray thoughts at all but represent the necessary action of a system dedicated to the very topic under discussion – the enlivening of the self. In other words, mind wandering appears to constitute an important function of the mind as it goes about being a doer doing. Again, in this essay, we seek to balance what can be learned from neuroscience and developmental research with what can be observed clinically. But a quick caution to the reader is certainly in order here: on the altogether new topic of "mind wandering," our third essay represents rather our first thoughts on the subject – not the last word.

The reader who may be familiar with some of our earlier work will no doubt feel entitled to an accounting of how we square our new appreciation for mind wandering with what we have previously written. To that end, we have appended an Afterword, in which we take up our theory of motivational systems and seek to explicate it vis-à-vis our exploration of the new and different realm of mind wandering. As part of that endeavor, we will revisit the diagrams of our most recent book and update them in terms of the new vistas opened up by current research on this topic.

Chapter 1

The First Year of Life

In this first essay we focus on the baby's early lived experience, specifically on the origins and early development of the sense of self – of the person as a doer doing with others. By being a doer we mean both acting and taking in, both initiating and responding to others and to oneself.

In the pages that follow, we will delineate developmental events that intersect and build toward the individual's sense of an agentic self. The upshot of these developmental processes is a sense of self that is embedded in bodily experience, intersubjective relations, and a historically determined cultural environment. Ultimately, we will highlight 12 developmental processes inherent in the emergent sense of self that subsequently play a significant role in our approach to therapy and our understanding of the basis of effecting positive change, two topics we will take up yet more thoroughly in our second essay. But here let us note at the outset that the effectiveness of these early processes in fostering an emergent, enlivened self in early life may be enhanced or diminished by positive or negative occurrences in subsequent development.

Postulations of a balance between agency and relatedness as aspects of self development already have an extensive history in recent analytic theory. In 1989, Lichtenberg proposed,

> Coherence of the core self . . . builds on the invariance of agency, especially volition and proprioceptive feedback. To this coherence is added a sense of self as a locus in space, as a source for temporal sequencing, and as the locus of particular rises and falls in intensity. Concurrently, the mother is experienced as a separate source of volition, of temporal sequencing (in vocal games), of intensity gradients, and of "form," especially the emotional communications of her face. Affect sharing is a part of lived experience from the earliest days of life, when neonates imitate mother's facial expressions, especially when she exaggerates them.
>
> (Lichtenberg, 1989, p. 25)

The observations and research findings we present in this essay can be seen as substantiating the proposals heralded in this passage from 1989.

The Creation and Development of a Sense of an Agentic Self

Being a "doer" and "doing with other and with self" entail experiences of oneself as motivated and as having intentions and goals. We encapsulate those experiences under the rubric of a "sense of an agentic self." Furthermore, we consider this "self" to involve two domains. One domain is experiential involving the incipient sense of self. It is important to observe at the outset that the experience of the self is not synonymous with conscious awareness. Lived experience encompasses both implicit and explicit modes. A doer doing with others and with self is under the constant influence of implicit as well as explicit modes of experience.

A second domain entailed in the formation of the agentic self involves neural processes that categorize, organize, stabilize, modify, integrate, and recategorize. Each of these two basic domains – the experiential self-system and the neural process self-system subtending it – would present an incomplete portrayal of development without the other. The gradual development and maturation of the system of neural networks make experiencing possible. As experiencing occurs, the maps and schemas of neural networks form and continuously undergo revision, and, as experiences repeat, the strength of the connections of the involved neural networks increases. We will follow the two domains, the thread of implicit and explicit experience and the thread of process that derives from the neural networks, and emphasize one or the other as each amplifies the creation of a sense of self in general, and the agentic sense of self in particular.

We contend that a full-term neonate has a "mind." The criteria on which we base this premise are that neonates experience affects, have perceptions, create images, form implicit memories, and discriminate among caregivers. Furthermore, neonates have processes that allow for the rapid categorizing and organizing of information. In addition, neonates and young infants seek and respond to familiar experiences while also being open to the activation of interest triggered by novelty. More than a decade ago, in their thought provoking chapter on "Early capacities and presymbolic representation," Beebe and Lachmann (2002) presented extensive research evidence as to the timing of developments that "provide us with a view of the infant as an astonishingly competent creature" (p. 65). "Competent" here refers to capacities that allow an infant to be a doer doing, initiating and responding, across a wide range of affects, intentions, and goals (motivational systems). The findings detailed in this essay and in contemporary infant research challenge and contradict the theory of primary narcissism and views of the infant as autistic, undifferentiated, grandiose, and omnipotent.

In the following sections we combine observational descriptions with research and theories that track the creation of the sense of self as an affective agent. Rather than offer a chronological presentation of development, in each of the sections we focus on one of the many facets of early development. We will organize this survey around a series of responses to the following questions, questions that taken together depict the integrative tapestry of emergent development in the first year of life.

1 What can be recognized about the emergence of a sense of an agentic self in the first minutes of a neonate's life?
2 What prenatal predispositions influence the neonate's experience of being a doer doing with others and with self?
3 As development proceeds, how are images categorized?
4 How do early preferences for a helper or giver and aversion to a hinderer or taker emerge? How do these preferences interact with the early origins of narrative capacity?
5 How does self-touch and being touched emerge? What does touch contribute to the dyadic system?
6 What groupings of experiences of intentions and goals (motivational systems) can be recognized early in infancy?
7 How does the experience of being a doer with affects and consciousness emerge?
8 How do thresholds for positive and negative affect activation become established?
9 How do infants acquire and develop the basic elements of speech?
10 What is the significance of the bidirectional mode of infant-caregiver interplay and the inferences and attributions that emerge?
11 How does being a socially competent doer emerge in infancy?
12 What is the infant's experience of being a playful doer doing in response to the invitations that come from the nonhuman environment: a ball is to throw, a teddy is to hug?
13 How do infants acquire the ability to be a doer who can both *initiate* interactions with others and *cooperate* with the initiatives of others?
14 Parallel with the trajectories for those infants developing a secure capacity for bidirectional initiating and cooperating, what are pathways that lead to disruptions of initiating and failures in cooperating?
15 What are the many processes that lead to the emergence and functioning of motivational systems, and how are motivational systems integrated with the sense of an agentic self?

4 The First Year of Life

16   What allows the agentic self to advance from the early modes of intentions and goals to the greater complexity of the verbal symbolic system and creativity? Here the focus will be on the essential role of metaphoric processes.

17   When the doer doing encounters obstacles, how do we understand the divergent pathways leading toward confidence and optimism or alternatively toward insecurity and pessimism? Here the focus is on what is traditionally called, following Tronick (2002), disruption-repair sequences, though we add to this, following Kohut (1977), the idea that repair involves the restoration of an empathically based relationship.

18   How do we understand early memory that interlocks with subsymbolic and imagistic symbolic processing and influences the trajectory for the doer's varied expectations, intentions, and goals?

19   What role do experiences of awe and admiration play in the doer's evaluation of others and self?

20   Summarizing from the prior sections, what lived experiences crucial for development in the first years of life are basic to the processes that subsequently facilitate therapy?

Again, each question and answer may be viewed as if one is looking through a prism at a particular aspect of development bearing on the sense of self. Our choice not to present a chronological account is in keeping with the complexity and plasticity of nonlinear dynamic systems. We hold that the traditional presentation of stages conveys a falsely linear perspective. Rather than occurring in fixed phases, we view development in terms of flexible, somewhat unpredictable trajectories of multiple pathways and outcomes. The enlivened self begins in infancy. But its trajectory is not a linear one.

Mrs. H

While the main thrust of the present discussion is to provide a view of the developments of the agentic sense of self through observations and research on the infant in the first year of life, we preface our examination of infancy by presenting an adult patient whose first year of life was reconstructed in a long and difficult analysis. Just as the concept of the enlivened self originates out of our therapeutic experiences, so, too, does our interest in early life. And this raises the issue of what exactly do we learn in the analysis of an adult that might enrich our curiosity about and appreciation for experiences of being a doer doing in very early development.

The patient in question, Mrs. H, has been chosen because so much of what emerged and was enacted and was revealed by her in the course of treatment dealt with her very early life experiences of success and failure in being an affective doer doing with others. To a striking degree the dispositional influences arising from Mrs. H's early life experiences could be linked to her adult successes and failures in being a doer doing.

Both development throughout life and progress in psychoanalysis are strongly influenced by framing contexts. The context for the narrative of Mrs. H's analysis is that the analyst, who is one of us (J. L.), was a candidate treating his first patient in a training institute that emphasized neutrality, abstinence, and anonymity, and oedipal conflict. The case supervisor was a strong advocate of the conservative approach, but fortunately was open to the significance of preoedipal development. The combination of the analyst's inexperience, uncertainty, and struggles with the constraining strictures placed on his responsiveness combined with the patient's intense needs in such a way as to create an ambiance of ongoing tension.

Now, fifty years after the termination of this analysis, the relational stresses can be seen to have constituted an implicit enactment that probably exaggerated the manifestations of Mrs. H's emotional pathology. Nonetheless, however exaggerated or caricatured these manifestation were, due to the framing context, what we found has a ring of authenticity supported by subsequent research and observations. (We are pleased to note that the initial paper, written for presentation in 1964 and based on Mrs. H's by then completed analysis, was entitled "On the vicissitudes of the early awareness of the self.")

Mrs. H came for analytic treatment because of a severe cancer phobia that gradually metamorphosed into a fear of becoming pregnant. In the initial consultative interview, she manifested immediately a heightened tension and difficulty in talking freely, a difficulty that became painfully characteristic of many subsequent sessions. Rather than being volunteered in a conversational, spontaneous flow, information was provided in a burst of words in response to a specific question. Her only comment that had a ring of spontaneity and intensity in the first interview occurred toward the end when I asked her if there was any important person in her life she had not spoken of. She replied: "No. I have a twin. She is 10 minutes younger. I never let her forget it. I bossed her all the time. I was always the smart one – she the pretty one." During the next four-and-a-half years of treatment, she elaborated on this theme: She did better in school; she forced her sister to give her a favorite doll; she was energetic and her sister lazy; she was better at sewing, cooking, managing money, and had married first.

These early years of analytic work were also marked by persistent silences; on one occasion the silence lasted for seven consecutive hours. Mrs. H's silences were accompanied by a parallel constraint on my part that I felt I was required to maintain. Additionally, she isolated daily events, and events occurring during sessions, and kept herself fixed to these items shorn of any connections to

6 The First Year of Life

larger contexts. Yet she would simultaneously feel guilty, depressed, and hopeless about her defensiveness. This picture of a tense, inhibited, laconic, depressed, embarrassed, shame-faced woman contrasted completely with her usual personality. Outside the analysis, as she described herself and reported being viewed by others, she was generally garrulous, gossipy, aggressive, energetic, and flirtatious.

She treated each issue of the arrangements – hours, fee, and so on – as a struggle for domination. Whatever the decision, she would briefly rail against it or bear it in pained, victimized silence, but what her feelings might mean was never to be discussed. The prototypic interaction was that nothing could be discussed or negotiated as though between well-intentioned equals. A matter in dispute was settled by the instantaneous, often unconscious judgment that she or the other person was being mean, unjust, impatient, and dogmatic, and nothing further could or needed to be said about it.

A major turning point occurred unexpectedly in the fifth year. By this time we had been able to connect her fear first of cancer and then of pregnancy with her belief that her body, like her mother's, was fragile. During the mother's pregnancy with Mrs. H and her twin the mother had been quite ill. The twins were born prematurely and spent three months in an incubator. Subsequently they were cared for by multiple caregivers while the mother recovered. Another issue was Mrs. H's doubts about her ability to regulate either retention or expulsion, the difficulty being based on early and premature efforts at toilet training. By this time in the treatment, although Mrs. H vigorously denied any benefit from the analysis, she experienced many gains in her outside life. Particularly noteworthy was the following: She had discontinued contraceptive use, become pregnant, and with no difficulty had given birth to a daughter.

A year and some months afterward, when her daughter was 16 months old, Mrs. H began to talk anxiously about her daughter's play with another child of the same age. As she talked about the aggressive elements in their play, to my surprise I recognized that she identified strongly with the underdog. Her poignant feeling for the child's losing possession of a toy or being pushed around was in stark contrast to the manner in which she usually talked about rivalry. From this, I inferred that the patient had blocked awareness of all memory of a period when her twin sister, and not she, had been the dominating one. Prior to this, the only reference to Mrs. H not having consistently bested her twin was a brief statement that, while the sister had been a better reader in the first grade, Mrs. H had worked hard and soon moved into the best reading group.

Catching up and overtaking proved to be a prototype for her entire early development. Mrs. H, the older by 10 minutes, but by two pounds the smaller of the premature twins, had been slower in maturation than her larger sister. She had been less able

The First Year of Life 7

to comply with efforts at feeding and at premature toilet training, spoke later and less well, and was the loser in early scraps with her sister. As soon as she could, by the third and fourth year, she used her energetic nature to struggle and scramble ahead in every area, including talking. Her narratives of how she bested her twin were often accompanied by a burst of uncontrolled laughter at her sister's discomfort. Interpretations of the meaning of the laughter, especially its fragmentary appearances in the transference, led Mrs. H to a full recognition of her sadistic enjoyment of turning the tables on someone, of frustrating the frustrator. Its opposite, being the disadvantaged one of a pair, was felt by the patient as a painful humiliation.

Only with great difficulty could Mrs. H come to recognize and accept the detrimental influence on her current relationships of her tendency to experience polar alternative positions of, at one extreme, being the humiliated underdog, and, at the other extreme, being the one who overcomes and enjoys it sadistically. The fear of reexperiencing the humiliation of her early struggles with her twin led her to avoid challenges. She feared she might be as unsuccessful as she had been in the first years – that is, she might revert to the "I am the one who can't talk" role as she did early in the analysis. Her mood was also affected. The mother's responses exacerbated the differences between the twins. She was more giving to the cheerier, less finicky, larger twin, and less so to my patient, whose contrasting tendencies, so like the mother's, were a mixture of shared depression and disapproval.

The silences during Mrs. H's analysis took on varied meanings at different times. From the standpoint of interpretive practice during the period in which the treatment was conducted, silence was regarded primarily as a manifestation of defense. Viewed as we would now, through the lens of motivational systems theory, each experience of silence could have been regarded as an expression of a particular intention and goal. When Mrs. H used silence as a means of withdrawal from shame, self-defeat, and humiliation, it served aversive and self-protective functions. When she was angry and withholding, the silence was motivated by a need to react antagonistically in the face of a belief that she was being abandoned by my silent disapproval. When she felt pessimism and a lack of agency, especially in the absence of an empathic response from me, she reexperienced the hopelessness of "I am the twin who is yet incapable of talking." But she could also utilize the "I can't talk" role to assert a perverse power through sadistic defiance. There were yet other variations. Particularly when the analysis began proving helpful, some silences took on a more positive quality. In these silences, Mrs. H experienced a respite, an opportunity to just be, to let her nontasked mind wander, while she replenished her energy in a quiet place with a controlled temperature and an accepting other. These replenishing mind-wandering silences occurred particularly after periods when she had been hectically scurrying about being the energetic, capable one. In these instances the silences were motivated by a need for physiological regulation combined with activating a sense of an attachment connection to a nondemanding, noncritical caregiver. Silences also occurred at times when she was coping with a planned separation and served as a means for her to gather herself together to adapt to the time apart.

A puzzling phenomenon involved Mrs. H's perception of me. On several occasions outside of the office, at times and places where she could have expected to see me, she looked straight at me, but persistently and totally denied that she had seen me. On entering or leaving the office, she avoided looking directly at me. The major source of her selective blindness was her fear, nay her conviction, that I thought her worthless and couldn't stand another minute of her lack of associative productivity. She was certain that this was all to be seen in my facial expression. Only through darting glances at me when entering or leaving the office could she obtain any glimmer of reassurance. Paradoxically, if I spoke to her about a practical arrangement, she would look at me full face and experience a relief that approached elation regardless of whether the content of what I said was pleasing or more likely the source of a coming dominance struggle. Content aside, our full face interchange broke through her fixed unconscious belief that we were reliving her experience of being with a disapproving, frustrated, depressed mother, and her own shameful inability to alter the stuck nature of that pairing. Additionally, the contrast with the repetitive unfolding before her eyes of the more successful pairing of her mother with her twin made visual perception a source of painful expectations.

In a later phase of the analysis another source of the negative expectation that she would be viewed unfavorably came from the analysis of a dream in which a man suddenly rose up in the middle of a room. Working with the dream led to the recovery of her memory of being erotically aroused on first seeing me enter the waiting room for the initial consultative hour. The pleasurable nature of that experience was immediately converted to painful humiliation by her thought – mentioned at the end of the initial consultative session – that her twin was the pretty one, an evocation in the sensual/sexual sphere of all the other early expectations of being viewed unfavorably.

A particularly puzzling symptom that occurred intermittently throughout the analysis was what Mrs. H referred to as "yawning." Like ordinary yawning, this recurrent phenomenon entailed a compulsive opening of her mouth. But unlike ordinary yawning, the main feature was that once her mouth was open she did not feel she could voluntarily close it. Also unlike ordinary yawning, when it occurred she did not suck air in. The phenomenon seemed to both of us to be a manifestation of anxiety but otherwise escaped explanation. Based on the understanding that finally emerged, I would say looking back on it from today that often she was responding to her perception of an empathic failure on my part. As Mrs. H became less anxious in the last year of analysis, the open mouth experience seemed to have disappeared. Then in a session about two months before termination, after a second successful pregnancy and birth, she related that her older daughter asked if she could give the bottle to the 3-month-old baby. As Mrs. H related how the little girl was unable to hold the bottle steady on the baby's lips, and before Mrs. H. could tell me that the nipple went in too far, I found myself modeling the symptom of having my mouth open and being obstructed from being able to close it. As I started to describe my understanding, Mrs. H experienced the same open O-shaped mouth symptom. She then remembered that she had been told by her older sister that often their mother would feed the more rapidly responsive twin while having the older sister feed the slower, more finicky baby. The open mouth experience was a somatic marker of both the pragmatic ineptness of the child feeder and the preferential abandonment that was frequently repeated especially in the early years. It went along with the transference belief that I didn't want to be bothered with her and would have preferred another. Especially in the early period of the analysis, this implicit attribution was frequently actualized in the underlying enactment that characterized many of our silences and dominance transactions. In these moments she was the baby who couldn't or wouldn't, and I was the caregiver who was puzzled, inept, and would have preferred to be working with an easier analysand. But with her following her childhood model, and I separately mine, neither of us would accept a defeated pessimistic stance but would and did struggle successfully to persevere.

Since much of my understanding of Mrs. H was based on a reconstruction of the early preverbal period, with all the hazards of error that involved, I was reassured by confirmatory findings from Dorothy Burlingham's (1949) direct observation of twins. Burlingham writes:

> It was possible to observe that the twins, at an early age, were aware of the differences in their achievements. The less advanced of the twins noticed that the other was able to crawl, kneel and stand while he himself was only able to lie or sit, and was upset as he watched the activities of the other. . . . This forces the less active child to compete with the active one at a much earlier age than is usual in children. The competitive situation will again be increased through the relationship to the mother or nurse. The spontaneous admiration

they receive from the mother for each new accomplishment causes pleasure. The more backward child not only observed the accomplishment of his twin but also the expression of pleasure the mother shows.

(p. 62)

Burlingham describes the dissatisfaction of the subordinate twin and documents two reactions: First, the dominated twin immediately took advantage of any reduction of greater strength or activity of his twin to take the lead, and, second, the subordinate twin would take obvious delight in knocking down his more advanced sister or brother.

In thinking about Mrs. H's earliest experiences, three issues readily present themselves as having important clinical applications pertaining to the experience of the self. All three can be readily tied to early development, not just in Mrs. H's case but across the board. Each of these aspects of early development has a life-long impact on the sense of an affective agentic self. Each of these developmental lines also has particular salience for clinical work.

First, thresholds for the activation of affective states and moods exert an implicit influence on the sense of self and on the success or failure of therapeutic approaches. (For example, Mrs. H's early arising dysphoric states were doubtless exacerbated by the "neutral" and "abstinent" therapeutic frame surrounding her treatment.) Second, being the recipient of attributions, especially in the formative years, and making attributions about others and oneself in turn, is significant for identity themes, transferences, and countertransferences. (For example, Mrs. H relived being regarded as the difficult one who couldn't talk and her twin as the pretty one who was easy.) Sequences of disruption and repair with subsequent restoration of empathic relatedness, considered in both their individual but especially their cumulative effect, exert an implicit and explicit influence on the doer's confidence in his or her ability to recover from the inevitable disjunctions in intentions and from the messiness of empathically based and other communications in treatment. (For example, Mrs. H's exquisite sensitivity to the disruptive impact of empathic failures on her confidence as a doer showed repeatedly in the treatment, as did her resilience in terms of her proclivity to turn the tables as a form of repair.)

At the end of this essay, we will expand the list of clinically important aspects of the early development of the self to a total of 12 items. But first let us tackle the questions we have posed about the emergence of a sense of self in the first year of life.

The Emergence of a Sense of Self

1 What can be recognized about the emergence of a sense of an agentic self in the first minutes of a neonate's life?

J. L. described the first minutes of his granddaughter Katie's neonatal life (Lichtenberg, 2008). After a normal delivery, Katie emerged with a robust cry that continued as the nurse briefly held her on the examining table. The nurse handed her to me, and as I held her firmly while gently rocking her and speaking to her comfortingly, Katie's cry lowered to a whimper. I placed her on her mother's chest and instantly (presumably hearing the familiar heartbeat) Katie quieted. I asked my daughter, Ann, if she wanted to initiate a "feeding," knowing that milk might not flow but that even so, a "dry run" would be facilitative. My daughter said yes and asked me to position Katie. I moved Katie's head to the nipple, chucked her cheek to trigger seeking and sucking. As Katie began to suck, the nipple now firmly in her small mouth, both mother and baby seemed to glow in harmony.

We hypothesize that each activity Katie originated had an experiential quality of agency. By that we mean that it combined an emotion, intention, and a goal. The experience of agency is an emergent quality of a proto-self, an emergent quality in which the infant experiences himself or herself as an initiator and responder, as a doer and as doing with others and with self. These are the processes we infer are operating when we observe Katie acting and responding.

When Katie responded first to comforting by me and then to the touch of her mother's skin and the sound of Ann's heartbeat, we infer that she experienced and categorized a trace of a sense of a doer doing. The doing is both with "other" (a holding environment) and with self – downregulating a negative affect state. We imagine that the doing included the diminishing of the aversive affect state, responsiveness to skin touch, and recognition of and responsiveness to a familiar rhythmical sound. When Katie responded to the rooting reflex being triggered, as she placed her mouth on the nipple, she began her sucking activity. We propose that she then experienced and categorized an additional trace of a sense of doer doing. This doing included purposeful self-regulating coordination of movements of head, lips, mouth, and sucking with the activation of mutual sensual enjoyment.

In these complex interactions, simultaneous with her active doing, Katie experienced receiving first my and then her mother's holding, cradling, and being spoken to softly. We assume from her actions and responses that Katie experienced a sense of being valued and of being able to self-activate what was needed. These

12 The First Year of Life

experiences contribute to forming an incipient sense of self-worth and general optimism about being safely in the world.

Viewed from a perspective of the body, we identify activities that are physiological, sensory, and motor. From a perspective of the brain, we identify processes involving neural networks and centers such as the limbic system, sensory cortices, and amygdala, as well as decreases and increases in endorphins, cortisol, and so on. Viewed from the standpoint of the mind, we address experience whether nonconscious or in the core or primary consciousness. Experience in our usage is the ever-changing continuous creation of perception, cognition, affect, memory, and recursive awareness systems.

The Katie and Ann example places the nascent sense of self or proto-self within the context of continuous variable input from the body and relationships – an embodied relational mind creating a feeling, agentic, and valued sense of self. The interchanges in the vignette are indicative of an embodied relational mind "centered on the belief that cognitive processes are deeply grounded in modes of engagement with and action on the world, including those involving the body" (Vivona, 2009, p. 1330).

Action on the world, even in these very early stages, involves both the doing with and taking in from the environment, and the doing with and receiving of sensations from the body. The doing and responding with others and the doing and responding with and to one's body become categorized as distinguishable experiences of the agentic self. The relational doings and the perceptual sensory functions that support them become categorized as out there, external, other, close or distant, safe or dangerous, appealing or aversive. Acting on the body and the sensations that invite the actions and result from them become categorized as in there (mouth, ear, nose, stomach, bladder), on there (skin, head), contained in or expelled from, pleasurable or painful, sensual, or orgasmic, in motion or at rest. Feinberg (2009) refers to

> an interoself system that is concerned with the internal milieu and homeostatic needs of the organism. The products of processes generated by the interoself system are experienced as feelings coming from within the organism itself. As a result these feelings . . . are experienced as belonging to the internal and personal self. The exterosensorimotor system is devoted to the organism's interactions with the environment, those sensations from and actions generated toward the external world.
>
> (p. 157)

The First Year of Life 13

Llinas (2001) implicates the internalization of movement and the generation of intrinsic images as providing an internal context or disposition that permits sensory input from the external world to gain significance.

In summary, beginning in infancy and continuing throughout life, processing experience into categories of actions with and on the environment, and with and on the body, is essential to the overall sense of an agentic self. The category of doing to and sensing the body provides a sense of locus for doings to and receiving from the external world. Growing awareness of bodily self experience is fundamental to a grounded sense of reality (on the testing of reality from the standpoint of the body self, see Lichtenberg, 1978). However, the categories of interior and exterior as applied to the sense of self-agency are loose assemblies. As it emerges, the metaphoric process finds rich opportunities to bridge these boundaries, frequently using images of inside and outside to represent the other in dreams, poetry, and ordinary language.

This brings us to an important issue, which is not about infancy per se but about the kind of model of mind, of mental processing, that we are employing to conceptualize an agentic sense of self. In order to build a conceptual map of the lived experience of self in the act of being a doer doing with others and with self, and a receiver processing information from others and from self, our observations need to be informed by a conceptual understanding of the modes of information processing underlying the moment-to-moment interactive lived experiences of infants. The following list of our assumptions is offered as a preliminary summary to orient the reader to the modes of mental organizing via subsymbolic and symbolic imagistic encoding that guide our conceptions.

First, as already stated, a core aspect of the sense of self organizes and stabilizes around the sense of being a doer doing with others (initiating and responding).

Second, survival and reward neural networks, neural networks regulating homeostasis, and neural networks of the primary sensory cortices as well as subsymbolic and imagistic symbolic modes of encoding (Fosshage, 2005, 2011) are functional at birth. The emergence of REM sleep in utero offers strong support for the hypothesis that imagistic symbolic encoding in its earliest form is online at birth (Fosshage, 2011).

Third, the sense of an agentic self emerges via subsymbolic (Bucci, 1997) and imagistic symbolic (Bucci, 1985; Fosshage, 1983; Paivio, 1971, 2007) processing. Seeking similarities of lived experience and recognizing dissimilarities (entailed in metaphoric processing [Modell, 2006]) are central features of subsymbolic and imagistic symbolic processing (as well as later verbal symbolic processing).

Subsymbolic and imagistic symbolic encoding is involved in categorizations, comparisons, and computations as well as implicit memory that process complex functioning in infancy and throughout life.

Fourth, seeking, recognizing, and categorizing similarities of affects, intentions, and goals create motivational systems with core similarities. Elsewhere we have identified seven motivational systems based on core similarities. While in its core aspects each motivational system is distinct, we recognize many experiential aspects that overlap from one motivational system to others.

There is more to be said on all these points, but let us focus for a moment on subsymbolic and imagistic processing, since both are paramount in the first year of life. Subsymbolic processing is often nonconscious though it may also be at the edge of core or primary consciousness in infancy and indeed throughout life. Subsymbolic processing is nonlinear rather than sequential and uses parallel distributed neural networks rather than combining discrete elements (Bucci, 1997). Subsymbolic processing often functions rapidly, for example, in making quick spatial and motor adjustments and often conveys a sense of here-and-now immediacy to the agentic self.

For its part, imagistic encoding uses all sensory modalities to register and process information (Fosshage, 1983, 1997b; Paivio, 1971, 2007). Affective cognitive processing using imagistic encoding occurs during sleep in the form of dreaming beginning in utero during the last trimester. Following birth, utilizing imagistic and later verbal encoding, REM sleep processes information and enhances learning and very likely contributes to the establishment of neural memory networks (Fosshage, 1983, 1997b; Meissner, 1968; Reiser, 1990).

In infancy, subsymbolic and imagistic symbolic processing undergo a rapid transition as infants absorb, integrate, and synthesize stimuli – that is to say information – from their body and from their relational interactions. The rapid integration of information based on the lived experience of unfolding intentions and goals coincides with the rapid growth of interconnecting reentry and second-order neural networks that will provide the pathway for subsequently bootstrapping into symbolic processing and extended or higher-order consciousness (Edelman, 1992).

As we go along in this discussion we will explore the range of developmental outcomes by laying out a foundation of adaptive pathways and drawing parallels with problematic pathways. We recognize the potential for many turning points in the trajectory of normal and pathological pathways, turning points that are often unpredictable in their emergence and in the direction of their outcome. We will also detail steps in the transitions that occur during the neonate-to-older-infant developmental period, particularly those that advance the adaptive quality and complexity of infants' systems of intentions and goals.

2 What prenatal predispositions influence the neonate's experience of being a doer doing with others and with self?

Moving from the abstract proposals of the prior discussion, we now consider evidence of lived experience and subsymbolic and imagistic symbolic processing in the prenatal period. In our view, developments during the prenatal period cast a dispositional shadow on the regulation of the emerging motivational systems and the proto-self.

Before the era of research on intrauterine and neonatal experience the prior theoretical account we have just given would have appeared ridiculously adultomorphic. However, in intrauterine life a full-term neonate can have the experience of perceptual, cognitive, memory, and affective activation. These intrauterine developments make possible the nascent sense of doing or proto-self that we described as experienced by 5-minute-old Katie. Ultrasound studies (Piontelli, 1987) indicate that "long before birth a fetus can hear, respond to pressure and touch, swallow and taste, react to pain, choose its preferential position and have some kind of primitive dream experience and show the beginnings of some form of learning" (p. 454). In *Symptoms, Inhibitions and Anxiety*, Freud (1959) wrote: "There is much more continuity between intra-uterine life and earliest infancy than the impressive caesura of the act of birth allows us to suppose. What happens is that the child's biological situation as a fetus is replaced for it by a psychical object-relation to its mother" (p. 138).

Piontelli (1987) describes the intrauterine experiences of Gianni and Guilia. Mrs. B, Gianni's mother, had suffered having her second pregnancy end in a stillbirth due to *abruptio placentae*. Throughout her third pregnancy, with Gianni, Mrs. B's anxiety about losing her fetus pervaded her life. Gianni "remained immobile, tightly crouched in a corner of the womb, with his hands and his arms screening his eyes and his face, and his legs . . . tightly folded and crossed" (p. 460). Birth by Caesarian section was made difficult by his being so crumpled in a corner of the womb; the obstetrician had trouble pulling him out. After birth he was often immobile. He sucked slowly at the breast, frowning with his eyes closed. He would cling for hours to the breast. While nursing, his mother never looked at him but continued to talk to others. At one year, Gianni could crawl but preferred to sit in a corner holding the same toy.

In a different mother-fetus pair, Guilia, as she was observed in utero, floated most of the time in the amniotic fluid following the lulling rhythm of her mother's breathing. She occasionally rocked herself to sleep, but her most frequent activity was playing with her tongue, moving it in and out of her lips. On two occasions

16   The First Year of Life

she was observed wildly licking the placenta. Mrs. A, Guilia's mother, was a large, overweight woman with a warm smile and a calm, detached manner. After a wanted and uneventful pregnancy, Mrs. A had a difficult birth experience while her little Guilia seemed unperturbed by it all. The next day, when her mother tried to introduce her nipple, Guilia licked vigorously instead of sucking. Subsequently, feedings were times of rapid, furious sucking followed by Guilia returning to playing with her tongue. When solids were introduced at 4 months, Guilia ate so voraciously that at 10 months she weighed as much as a 2-year-old. Mrs. A noted that Guilia went wild when she heard a man's voice: "She is really a little whore . . . she is mad about men" (Piontelli, 1987, p. 459).

Here is how we understand the differences between Gianni and Guilia. In the womb, Gianni's aversive withdrawal was established as a protective immobility and led to restrictions on his experiencing traces of being a doer doing. After birth, the dyadic interplay of Mrs. B's avoidant, aversive attachment to Gianni, and his to her, added further to the dominant organization of Gianni's proto-self as a sad, frightened, devitalized clinger. Piontelli notes that on a rare occasion if Gianni's mother was responsive or he was with a babysitter or his father, he could relax and be less dysphoric.

In the womb, Guilia's lulling, rocking, playing with her tongue, and sucking established her strong dispositional inclination to experience traces of being a doer doing as a seeker of sensual enjoyment heavily centered on her mouth. After birth, the interplay of her mother's obesity and sexual preoccupation added further to the dominance of Guilia's proto-self as an excitable, overeating, sensually centered, endless rocker who "loved to have someone's arm between her legs" (Piontelli, 1987, p. 243).

Following Damasio (1994, 1999), we believe that the implicit memory of lived experience, however early in development the memory occurs, organizes enduring dispositions. Piontelli's compelling examples point to a hard-to-distinguish combination of nature and nurture that influences the unfolding of a doer doing and the qualities of the ensuing sense of self. The nature-nurture interplay is strongly suggestive but hard to evaluate.

The Imagistic Aspect of Lived Experience

3 As development proceeds, how are images categorized?

Representational images of being a doer doing use all sensory modalities. Very early images, schemas, or maps are categorized and recategorized and give the sense of self a cross-modal richness. In our use of the term *images*, we include maps and schemas and consider these terms to be equivalent.

In *Psychoanalysis and Motivational Systems: A New Look* (Lichtenberg, Lachmann, & Fosshage, 2011), we proposed that the foundation for motivational systems lies in the functioning of perceptual, cognitive, memory, affective, and recursive awareness systems. Affects, intentions, and goals and the sense of self as a doer doing with others emerge from the activation of these fundamental systems. And each emergent lived experience of intentions and agency dispositionally influences subsequent lived experiences. Expectations from prior experience tilt the direction of perception, cognition, and affects probabilistically, not concretely.

Consider the lived experience of Katie and other infants. They can't tell us in words or draw pictures so we must surmise from what they tell us in facial expression, eye and body movements, vocalizations, physiological activity, preferences, and state changes. Considerable evidence (Damasio, 1994, 1999) supports the view that an infant's lived experience coordinates inner and external perceptions of body sensations comprised of visual, auditory, gustatory, olfactory, and tactile and proprioceptive stimuli into images. Unlike the older child and adult who piece together discrete images and coordinate these images with words, an infant's imagistic experience is holistic and immediate. The holistic quality is made possible by neural networks that coordinate sensory stimuli across sensory modes together with the registry of felt and observed movement activity by mirror neurons (Rizzolatti, Fogassi, & Gallese, 2004).

The coordination of sensory and motor activity allows infants to simulate patterns of actions of others in conjunction with comparable activities and intentions of their own. A powerful consequence is that when infants are in an agentic mode, whether doing, imagining, or observing an activity while sensing their own intentions, they can rapidly, nonconsciously, infer the intention behind the activity of others. If the infant could articulate the nonconscious inferring of intentions, it might sound like this: "I turn my head, fix my gaze, and adjust my body intending to look at you, mother. When you turn your head, fix your gaze, adjust your body, you must intend to look at me." Or, "Smiling, mother reaches out to pick me up. I infer her intention to be affectionate – an intention implicit in an image I formed from repeated experiences of her picking me up affectionately. I eagerly adjust my body to be picked up. Mother and my intentions and emotions as I imaged them are concordant." Or, "I want to continue to play," in which case, "Our intentions are discordant." Or, "My tummy aches; I am cranky – I don't want to be picked up. I arch my back and resist."

The multitude of events in the moment-to-moment lived experience of infant and caregiver requires a process of cross-modal sensory and bidirectional motor activity. Images and memories form. Expectations emerge. Dispositions to search, seek, and react are created. From the images, memories, expectations, and dispositions,

18 The First Year of Life

inferences by the infant about his or her intentions and those of others become affective guides to an experiential appreciation of the doings and goals of self and others. This processing involves comparator functions (Stuss, 1992). These distinguish similarities and dissimilarities in patterns of repeated sensory and motor activities and emergent affects, intentions, and goals. Through these comparator functions similar affects, intentions, and goals and associated mental states are categorized and recategorized into motivational systems. While the nature and quality of early lived experience and the timing of developmental events such as forming inferences about intentions is often conjectural, the particular grouping of experiences and processes that come to be categorized into motivational systems can be recognized early (see question 6).

4 How do early preferences for a helper or giver and aversion to a hinderer or taker emerge? How do these preferences interact with the early origins of narrative capacity?

In a series of studies, Hamlin, Wynn, and Bloom (2007, 2010; Hamlin, Wynn, Bloom, & Mahajan, 2011) explored the developmental origins of the capacity of very young infants to evaluate and distinguish between the positive and negative behaviors of being helped or hindered. The experimenters based their approach on the knowledge that infants evidence a clear capacity to make discriminations based on preferences. For example, infants give positive responses to physically attractive faces and to making eye contact with familiar people. They give negative responses to angry or still faces. Infants at 3 months indicate a positive preference by looking while infants at 5 months indicate positive preferences both by looking and by reaching for.

In an experiment 3- and 6-month-old infants are exposed to two scenes with opposite outcomes. In both scenes the infants observe an incline and a block of wood figure with large googly eyes, "the climber," who initially is at rest at the incline's base. The climber then climbs to a lower plateau and does a jiggle-up-and-down dance of joy. The climber then attempts twice to reach the upper plateau, each time falling back to the lower plateau. Then the scenes diverge. In one, as the climber makes a third attempt, another figure enters the scene. This figure, the helper, gives the climber two bumps up. The climber reaching the top does another dance of joy. In the second exposure the climber again is making a third attempt to go from the first plateau to the top of the incline. This time the entering figure, a hinderer, gives two bumps that push the climber down resulting in a tumble end-over-end to the bottom.

The First Year of Life   19

In a second version of helper-hinderer scenes, 8-month-old infants observe a duck puppet struggling to open a transparent glass case enclosing an attractive rattle. The duck is either aided by an elephant puppet that holds the top open or hindered by an elephant puppet that sits on the top of the case. In a third variant, a duck puppet drops a ball and another puppet retrieves it. The duck gestures to get the ball back. The other puppet in one sequence gives it back. In another sequence the other puppet takes it.

In each age group tested the results were consistent. The infants responded preferentially to the helper or giver and aversively to the hinderer or taker. Proof of the hypothesis that infants were reacting to an event construed as an animate interaction was obtained in that infants demonstrated no preference for inanimate objects (wood blocks without googly eyes) whether the wood block was going up or down hill. Another control was to have a "neutral" climber go up and down the hill without interacting with the pushing climber, helper, or hinderer. When exposed to combinations of a neutral (nonsocially interactive) climber and a helper or a hinderer, infants looked at and/or reached for the helper rather than the neutral climber and the neutral climber rather than the "antisocial" hinderer.

The capacity of infants to discriminate and respond differently to social behavior increases in complexity. At 5 months infants are exposed first to a scene portraying a helper or a hinderer and then a second scene portraying a giver or taker. In some of the second scenes pro- or antisocial roles are similar across scenes; in others the roles are reversed, with the figure that was the helper in the first scene now the hinderer. Five-month-olds respond to the pro- or antisocial behavior evidenced in the second scene regardless of the behavior of either figure in the prior scene. Whether the figure was a helper and giver or hinderer and taker in the first scene didn't carry over. What mattered was only how the figure behaved in the second scene. At 8 months, however, the prior context influenced the response in intriguing and complex ways: "Our 8-month-old infants assessed the global value of an action – their patterns of choice suggest that, in particular, they viewed a locally negative action as bad when directed toward a prosocial individual, but good when directed toward an antisocial individual" (Hamlin et al., 2011, p. 19933). That is, 8-month-olds look with favor on a figure that acts against a hinderer. This carries over into their behavior. In contrast to the younger infants who simply avoid an antisocial figure, a toddler exposed to an individual who violates the rules of a game or acts in another antisocial manner approaches the offending individual to direct a negative behavior toward them. Toddlers also generalize across behaviors: By one year, in play sequences infants regularly associated positive actions with other positive actions, such as helping with caressing, and negative actions with other negative actions, such as hindering with hitting.

Overall, we concur with the researchers' conclusions: First, the early developmental emergence of the capacity for social evaluation is an evolved biological adaptation. Second, "the ability to judge differentially those who perform positive and negative social acts may form an essential basis for any system that will eventually contain more abstract concepts of right and wrong" (Hamlin et al., 2007, p. 559). Third, the "nuanced social judgments and actions readily observable in human adults have their foundations in early developing cognitive mechanisms" (Hamlin et al., 2011, p. 19933).

We hypothesize that these findings identify a narrative capacity as an early developing cognitive mechanism that underlies the ability of infants to identify the social helper or antisocial hinderer. Forming a narrative organizes lived experience by encoding events in stories, scripts, schemas, or maps. A fascinating conclusion from these studies is that infants as young as 3 months can observe a scene and organize it into a visual story with an ethical dimension, a mini-morality play if you will, and remember it long enough to identify and react to a character as a preferred one or an aversive one. By 8 months infants can organize two narratives of prosocial or antisocial behavior – distinguishing and remembering the helper or hinderer and the giver or taker – and apply that information from a first to a second visual story. By 1 year, infants recognize similar qualities such as helping and caressing found in different event narratives.

The capacities for moral judgments and narrative formation contribute to the emergence of understanding social norms and enforcing them. "Children as young as 2–3 years understand the constitutive rules governing social rule games (games that are governed by explicit rules) and games of pretense (games that are governed by implicit rules)" (Rakoczy & Schmidt, 2013, p. 18). The 2- to 3-year-old children who quickly learned a board game would spontaneously protest, criticize, and then teach a third party who performed an act that violated the game's rules. For example, in a game scenario in which two young children play an invented game in which they pretend a stone is soap, they will protest against a third party who refuses to go along with the make-believe. Similar spontaneous criticism and teaching will be launched at someone who misuses tools, violates simple verbal usage, or doesn't respect property ownership. Children's learning, understanding, and internalizing the rules of social norms facilitate their ability to predict the actions and response of others and themselves across a widening spectrum of contexts, including ultimately a therapeutic experience.

The First Year of Life 21

5 How does self-touch and being touched emerge? What does touch contribute to the dyadic system?

When observing infants, we are generally so captivated by their eye contact, facial expressions, sucking activity, and generalized body movements that the more subtle nuances involved in self-touch and being touched are easily overlooked. When an infant, especially a distressed infant, is being held, cuddled, and rocked, caregiver touch is a well-recognized form of downward regulation. Playful caregiver touching, tickling, jostling, and tossing are likewise well-recognized forms of heightened arousal. The older infant's discovery of the heightening arousal from genital self-touch or thigh rubbing is an emergent property of the sexual side of the sensual/sexual motivational system. Less well recognized is how neonates and young infants use their hands to regulate moment-to-moment states of arousal – soothing down or heightening up. These lived experiences of self-touch and being touched blend into the sensual hum of caregiver-infant attachment ambiance. During mother-baby proto-conversation, mother's words, tone, facial expression, head, hands, and body movements convey an affect state that coordinates (preferably in a middle range) with the baby's vocal gurgles, head and body movements, and hand-to-skin touching. Through their hand-to-skin touching infants regulate their arousal state in a manner that facilitates their ability to remain in an optimal mode of secure attachment. The infant's developing a successful capacity for touch as a mode of regulating a dyadic interaction or when alone depends on the success of the interactive contingency of the mother-infant dyadic system. Caregiver and infant bring into the dyadic system each individual's greater or lesser capacities for regulating both the other and the self (see the comparison of little Cora and Peggy infra).

Beebe and her colleagues elaborate:

> In future secure dyads, as infant vocal affect is more positive, maternal touch patterns are more affectionate (and vice versa). And as infants touch more (from none, to one, to two-plus touch behaviors per second), maternal touch patterns are more affectionate. As maternal touch patterns are more affectionate, infant engagement is more positive (and vice versa).
>
> (Beebe et al., 2012, p. 357)

Outside of a dyadic interaction when alone, infant positive affect is concordant with positive vocalizing and increased self-touch and vice versa.

Secure infants' sense of being known (empathically appreciated) by their caregivers and by themselves emerges as an emotionally significant outcome of contingent touching and other modalities of communication. These infants may come

22 The First Year of Life

to expect: "I can count on you to share my feelings, to 'get' what I feel; I feel known by you. I know how your face goes, I know you. I know I can influence you to touch me more tenderly when I need it" (Beebe et al., 2010, p. 357). Our hypothesis is that the infant's sense of being known in a collaborative dialogue in which more self-touch and caregiver touch is concordant with positive affect and less touch with negative affect provides a model experience infants can carry over into periods when alone. The subsequent doing-with-self in the form of more or less self-touch in conjunction with positive or negative affects then permits the emergence of more self-regulation and more self-knowledge. It is as though the infant is saying, "I know (recognize) myself in my changing emotional states as I touch my skin and vocalize in different patterns. I formed this link while regulating exchanges with my mother. Now I can use it to know and regulate myself." In short, reciprocal mother-infant touch regulation facilitates infant self-touch regulation; infant self-touch regulation then becomes an important resource of the securely attached infant – and adult.

Alternatively as Beebe et al. (2012) have also shown, in future disorganized infants, mothers lower their touch coordination with infant touch. These mothers do not acknowledge increasing infant touch as a cue for their more affectionate tender touch. Accordingly, left too alone and separate in the realm of touch, future disorganized infants

> showed a touch dysregulation: (a) less touch across all modes (touching object, mother, or own skin; (b) specifically less touching of their own skin; (c) greater likelihood of continuing in states of 'no touch' and unable to rely on themselves to provide self-comfort through touch. . . . Getting "stuck" in states of no touch may disturb the infant's visceral bodily feedback.
>
> (Beebe et al., 2012, p. 365)

This is a possible source for later dissociative symptoms. To this we add that such a state is also a possible source for addictive use of drugs for self-regulation.

An additional negative outcome of the failure of mother and infant to engage in a collaborative dialogue including touch is that future disorganized infants "have difficulty in knowing, and feeling known by, their mother's minds as well as difficulty in knowing their own minds" (Beebe et al., 2012, p. 367). These infants and their mothers are unable to experience moments of sharing emotional states and the coordination of touch and other communications that are a component of sharing. The infant's "mother does not coordinate her affection-to-intrusive touch patterns with his frequency of touch, generating infant expectations that his mother does not follow him in his touch patterns by becoming more affectionate as he touches more (and vice versa)" (Beebe et al., 2012, p. 367).

All of these examples are from preverbal infants functioning via cross-modal imagistic symbolic processes. Older, verbal children and adults abstract these physical and emotional phenomena into word metaphors such as "I feel deeply touched" when an empathic relatedness has added to their sense of a meaningful attachment experience. Similarly, "that was touch and go" can refer to an experience of uncertainty and risk comparable to the ambivalently attached child's experience of uncertainty about being responded to positively or being ignored or rejected. Or the metaphor "I don't want you to touch me," combines rejecting both the physical overtures of another comparable to the avoidantly attached infant.

6 What groupings of experiences of intentions and goals (motivational systems) can be recognized early in infancy?

Multiple motivational systems begin to emerge in early infancy to a degree that allows us to recognize their rudiments fairly clearly in the infant's behavior: physiological regulation, attachment and affiliation, exploration, aversiveness, and loving and caregiving.

Physiological Regulation

In early infancy the motivational systems involved with the regulation of physiological requirements frequently are dominant. These early requirements come to include bodily sensations of hunger, thirst, elimination of urine and feces, tactile stimulation, movement, drowsiness, changes in equilibrium, and relief from pain. These sensations in turn combine with caregivers' ministrations to form images reflective of feeding, diapering, touching and being touched, moving toward and away, being readied for sleep, and hurting and being calmed and soothed. These images are not static percepts but are composites of ongoing shifting intentions and goals and associated inferences (Lichtenberg, 1989). For example, images of mother opening her blouse blends into exposed nipple and flows into sucking and so on. In infancy many images are not words or discrete percepts but action messages that are believed to activate mirror neurons (Rizzolatti et al., 2004). Some images, however briefly, take on the quality of simple narratives or event memories.

24 The First Year of Life

Attachment and Affiliation

When experiences of attachment seeking, finding, losing, and refinding are dominant, images emerge of matching of gaze, looking away, reaching, grasping, touching, and being touched, as well as body tensing and body drooping. The emergent images combine the experience of a sense of self as agent with a sense of the other as agent. Intentions build around the affective shift from seeking to finding, from the disruption of losing, or of mismatching in gaze and intensity, to the repair of the connection and relief from experiencing fear and loss. Infants are able to infer the bidirectional intention of each participant to read momentary shifts of goals of the other. It is not known when infants or older children are able to sense that their image is firmly held in the mind of another, or if they have a reflective awareness of holding the other. Mahler (1968) put object constancy at 3 years. When images of self and other do form and become retrievable as intentions unfold, the positive effect of mirroring, twinship, and idealization provides critical support for coherence of the emerging and developing sense of self. Rather than becoming a categorical organization having constancy, the development of an individual's sense of others (and of the self) is a gradual, nonlinear, and nuanced process that continues to evolve.

A 3-month-old infant engaged in communicative play with one parent will actively turn to engage the other parent (Fivaz-Depeursinge & Corboz-Warnery, 1999). Contrary to an earlier view that intimacy is sought exclusively with a primary caregiver, infants form attachments with available others. Consequently, a child's attachment-based imagery of the experience of self-with-other is not confined to a principal caregiver. The world map of infants includes the entire panorama of those who participate in their environment – parents, grandparents, siblings, servants, pets, and toys. Attachment seeking and finding of individuals combines with a sense of intimacy and familiarity with the significant others as an affiliate group – the broader "us" of the infant's world – all mapped, sought, and missed.

Exploration

When an infant explores a sight, a sound, a taste, a feel, or a smell, or the way to grab or hold a bottle, a toe, or a toy, the infant has an opportunity to experience a sense of agency, directly and powerfully. Supported by the sense of safety gained from the proximity of the caregiver, an infant will repeat exploratory efforts to refine the coordination an action requires. From this behavior we infer that the infant's goal is to achieve a self-experience of efficacy and competence. An image of the achieved effective experience of the exploratory pursuit carries over into subsequent reiterations with increasing self-confidence.

Aversiveness

When aversiveness predominates, infants in the first year form two types of images. When the infant's signals of distress – crying, fear face, frown, sad/shame face, disgust, irritability, drooping, pulling back, pushing away – are responded to in a timely manner, the image formed of self with caregiver will represent the state change from distress, via the responder, to relief and a positive affect. The passage from distress to relief in infancy provides imagery of metaphoric significance for the many subsequent disruption-restoration sequences. In contrast, when the distress state persists, infants retain images of experiences of failed agency with a sense of helplessness. Under these circumstances, shades of panic and rage are noted, intentions and goal become disorganized, and withdrawal and apathy may ensue.

Loving and Caregiving

Love, in its romantic, idealized, nonlustful form, gains its iconic imagery and sensual affective tonality from the cooing, wooing, touching, kissing, fondling, gazing, tickling, teasing, bouncing, rocking, and giggling bidirectional play between infant and others. As it happens, early psychoanalytic theory gave greater significance to the infant's self-sensual arousal than to interactive arousal. To be sure, infants' self-soothing, self-stimulating body and genital touching, mouthing and sucking of fingers and objects, fondling of soft toys and blankets, bouncing and rocking are important components of self-regulation. These activities promote a sense of agency and the expectation that one is able to create pleasure and vitality and regulate arousal tone. That is, they contribute to images of an agentic self. In addition, self-sensual arousal contributes to images of the infants' body and skin as a desirable source of giving and receiving sensuality. We propose that the two sets of images, those of the loving dyad and those of the lovable self, together establish a basis for later images of a prideful person who loves and is worthy of being loved. These same experiences of the loving dyad, especially when sensual soothing acts to relieve distress, form the core experiences for affectionate caregiving.

7 How does the experience of being a doer with affects and consciousness emerge?

Throughout our prior discussion, we have focused implicitly on affect. Only actions that are experienced as having an affective impact, in our view, have significance for the development of the sense of self. But we owe the reader an account of how affects and consciousness emerge in tandem in infancy. Here we focus directly on the relationship of nonconscious affects and the proto-self in earliest infancy and how they then generate the later affective experiences of core consciousness and an expanding sense of self.

Panksepp (1998) proposed a "proto-self" that is centered on an initially non-conscious experience of affects. Panksepp reasoned that affective experience in general constitutes a proto-experience of self, *since the overall state of the organism is affected.* Through the midbrain limbic system, the proto-self thus becomes a point of reference that compares changes in affective states. The changes of affect provide information vital to the infant without the requirement of conscious awareness. While centering his conception on affects, Panksepp identified centers for rage, fear, lust, and attachment seeking. He thus approximates our conception of aversive antagonism and withdrawal, sensuality, and attachment motivational systems in their primitive forms.

In a way similar to Panksepp's emphasis on affect, Stern (1985), in his account of an infant's basic level of a sense of a core self, identifies patterned inner qualities of feeling that "belong with other experiences of self" (p. 71). Stern, as do we, gives primacy to "*self-agency,* in the sense of authorship of one's own actions and non-authorship of the actions of others: having volition, having control over self-generated action (your arm moves when you want it to), and expecting consequences of one's actions (when you shut your eyes it gets dark)" (Stern, 1985, p. 71, italics original). Stern notes that self-experience includes being a locus of coherent integrated action, not only while moving but also when still.

In our view the transition from the fetus's and neonate's proto-self experience of momentary affective agency to an experience of a core sense of self is made possible by the infant's increasing ability to track regularities in the flow of events. The processes that allow infants to track regularities, categorize, form expectations, and draw inferences make possible what Stern calls a basic level of self-history. By that he means that the infant develops a continuity with the past "so that one 'goes on being' and can even change while remaining the same" (p. 71).

For Damasio (1994), as for us, the mind arises from activity in neural circuits shaped by evolution to continuously monitor the affective states of the organism in action. The representation of the organism is anchored in the body. The body "contributes a *content* that is part and parcel of the workings of the mind" (Damasio, 1994, p. 226, italics original). As Damasio states, "The self is a constantly reconstructed biological state; it is *not* a little person, the infamous homunculus, inside your brain contemplating what is going on" (p. 227, italics original).

Damasio (1999) distinguishes the experience of unconscious *emotion* (comparable to Panksepp's nonconscious affect and proto-self) from the experience of *feeling* that is the hallmark of core consciousness. For Damasio, core consciousness implies a consciousness of self, since feelings (not unconscious emotions) implicitly entail an awareness of self.

Stated in Damasio's terms, first-order neural maps represent changes in body state and second-order neural maps represent the pattern of neural activity at the emotion induction sites. "Core consciousness occurs when the brain's representation devices generate an imaged, nonverbal account of how the organism's own state is affected by the organism's processing of an object" (Damasio, 1999, p. 169). In Damasio's terms, the nonverbal image or scene of core consciousness includes an account of the object-organism relationship. That relationship is the source of the sense of self in the act of knowing. In our terms, the nonconscious experience of emotion and agency of the proto-self undergoes further developmental steps. These steps evolve into a feeling of self-agentic experience that includes the person's consciousness and reflective awareness. "Stepping into the light" is Damasio's evocative metaphor for core consciousness, for the emergence of the knowing mind, for the momentous transformation of a proto-self into a feeling, agentic, reflective experience of self. Damasio's sense of self in the act of knowing identifies recursive sensing as a fundamental process of a person's psyche. Second-level neurons register the ongoing processing by first-order neurons active in the proto-self period. In consequence, recursive sensing becomes increasingly complex. We regard the early recursive sensing and awareness to be the foundation for reflective awareness of one's own conscious experiencing as well as for empathically sensing the state of mind and intentions of others.

Edelman (1987, 1992, 1998) refers to the neonate's dawn of awareness as "primary consciousness." This process involves forming an ongoing complex scene. In turn, this scene is created by a current perception becoming linked with memories of a small group of evolutionarily based "values" (preferences) in the limbic system. For Edelman memory is not storage of information but an active process of categorizing associatively and continually recategorizing. Neural reentry is a critical process for Edelman's theory. Through reentry, categorizing, and recategorizing, each perception involves an act of creation and each memory involves an act of imagination. Reentry is a complex exchange of parallel signals between the neural maps or scenes that correspond to perceptual categories and the neural maps of actions, affects, memory, and cognition. Continual reentrant signaling creates perceptual categorization in real time, a scene in the here and now.

28   The First Year of Life

For both Damasio and Edelman consciousness is two-tiered. Core (Damasio) or primary (Edelman) consciousness is the neonate's and infant's here-and-now awareness. Extended (Damasio) or higher-order (Edelman) consciousness results from the older child's bootstrapping into a more complex level of symbolic imagery and language-centered symbolic processing with the potential for self-reflection and a biographic sense of past, present, and future. "Language or its neural precursor is required for the robust emergence of higher order consciousness, just as primary consciousness is required for the acquisition of language" (Edelman, 1987, p. 72).

8   How do thresholds for positive and negative affective activation become established?

With this question, we take up Tronick's concept of thresholds for affective activation waves and suggest an extension of his concept of positive or negative mood activation to other pairs of opposite affects. Along with Damasio's emotion induction sites, the activation of affective waves describes a process potentially responsible for the emotional component of many self-states.

Affective activation wave theory integrates intersubjective and intrapsychic lived experience with a process that gives an emotional tonal quality to an individual's approach to his or her intentions and goals. We propose that wave theory offers an explanation for whether the agentic sense of self inclines toward a positive, optimistic or negative, pessimistic orientation.

Drawing on the contributions of Sander (1983), Tronick (2002) hypothesized an explanation for the source of persistent or regularly recurrent moods such as feeling upbeat or depressed. Tronick suggests that the source of changes of mood lies in the changing amplitudes of positive or negative affect activation waves. He proposed that positive and negative lived experiences exert a constant influence on the affective activation waves. Positive and negative experiences impact the thresholds for the activation of subsequent positive or negative affective waves. A higher threshold implies that it takes a stronger trigger to activate the corresponding affect; a lower threshold means that an affect can be more readily triggered.

As an illustration, Tronick provides a compelling account of an infant's developing negative moods in the morning. Originally, his hypothetical infant's day begins with her being in a neutral affective state, open equally to positive or negative input. Then her unsmiling and critical mother appears, and the infant's negative activation wave increases in amplitude above the activation threshold. The infant goes into a negative state. "She has a pouty expression, whimpers, turns her head into the bedding and starts to suck her thumb. Within moments, more negative affective elements are recruited to this negative affective state. She starts to wail" (Tronick, 2002, p. 84). The mother shifts to a comforting stance, but the infant remains in a negative mood. The mother persists and the negative mood starts to weaken. Without further activation, the amplitude of the negative wave dissipates, while the soothing causes the amplitude of the positive wave to rise above its activation threshold. "She looks at her mother with big wide eyes, smiles, reaches up to her to be picked up. But the mother gets distracted and looks away, lost in thought" (p. 84). Rebuffed, the baby returns almost immediately to her negative affect state and remains in a negative mood until her nap. "The mother says to her husband, 'Boy was she in a mood this morning'" (p. 84).

Tronick identifies five factors that delineate the process by which the negative mood of this morning became the infant's negative mood on subsequent mornings: (1) Affective waves alter the threshold of their activation based on affective input. The negative affect induces the amplitude of the negative wave to remain at a heightened level close to the threshold. Consequently, during the small-scale waxing and waning of experience, small negative activations will have more impact than small positive activations, since the activation of the positive wave is farther from a threshold trigger. (2) Affect states tend to recruit and augment related affect triggers. The recruitment is a self-organizing process contingent on the infant's own negative affective behavior. Nonenvironmental augmentation of the negative wave activation can arise from the infant's pinched facial expression, clinched fist, abdominal discomfort, hunger, or memory of related experience. (3) The infant's negative affect tends to evoke a reciprocal negativity in the mother, resulting in mutual augmentation. "Perhaps she (the mother) thinks to herself, 'I just got more and more frustrated. I couldn't figure what pleased her'" (Tronick, 2002, pp. 85–86). (4) Recurrence of the negative experience increases all the factors consolidating their impact. The repetition of a pattern – an unresponsive face or prolonged unrelieved hunger or the parent's repeated morning distraction by family arguments or worries – creates the negative response over time. Once created, on each day the negative triggering requires less input and the arousal of a positive state requires a more intense activation. (5) Regulation via the biological clock fixes the repeated negative affective state into a temporal pattern. With the daily recurrence of a negative interaction on awakening, the ultradian and diurnal organization of the negative activation wave is modified, so the infant awakens in the morning with the amplitude of the negative activation wave already approaching threshold and a positive wave requiring considerable stimulation to activate. Morning becomes a reading in the biological clock by

30 The First Year of Life

which the negative mood state repeats the processes of the day before and the day before that.

One of us (Lichtenberg, 2005) has suggested an expansion of Tronick's wave activation theory to affects other than the mix of depression, irritability, and anger. Tronick's theory describes a process by which repetitive and prolonged states of depression result in lower wave activation thresholds so that a depressive mood is easily activated. In contrast, the less frequent experience of a happy state results in a higher wave activation threshold requiring much greater stimulation to lift the mood. However, other paired affects demonstrate similar reciprocal regulatory potential. Affection and contentment or anger and irritability, interest triggered by novelty or boredom triggered by too much repetition, courage and confidence or doubt and fear, also have the wave-like characteristics of waxing and waning with the altering of thresholds for activation. Very early in life, some infants and young children may experience, recruit, and augment positive affective wave activation that contributes to an ongoing, possibly life-long, optimistic confident sense of self-agency. Alternatively, other less fortunate infants and young children may have repetitively altered thresholds for negative affective wave activation leaving them disposed to depression, anger, and shame and/or anxiety as well as a sense of impaired agency. The closer negative affective experiences are to activating neural survival centers the more likely repetition will have a traumatic effect. As a result, responses to related stimuli will become more concretized and automatic. They will also be more difficult to alter in response to positive experience.

Working clinically with patients with persisting negative moods such as Mrs. H, we ordinarily attempt to identify the triggering contexts in and out of the treatment that occupy the immediate foreground. Nonetheless we sometimes sense how both patient and analyst have to struggle against a background pull, an undertow of a mind burdened by depression, or irritability, or anxiety, or shame and humiliation, all of which was true of Mrs. H. Understanding the background pull or undertow as the result of a low threshold for the activation of the particular negative affect wave coupled with a high threshold for the activation of a positive affective wave offers an explanation for puzzling constraints on the ameliorative effect of empathy-based interpretation.

The Sense of Self With Others

With the following questions, we turn to the proto-self's nascent capacities for interaction. As language will eventually become central in doing with others, we begin by presenting evidence for the evolutionary-based linking of the experience of hearing and processing human speech that builds neural networks of speech elements. The early recognition of affective verbal communication solidifies the sense of the self as locus for feelings, intentions, and goals. The processing of verbal elements integrates the existing gestural communication of proto-self with the developing agentic sense of self as simplified verbal communicator. The rapid acquisition of vocabulary leads to a self fully capable of linguistic communication to and with others and self (see Litowitz, 2011).

9 How do infants acquire and develop the basic elements of speech?

In the womb and out, babies are bathed in the sound of human speech. This leads to a critical question: Since the infant can't conceptualize the meaning of the speech, does the ubiquity of speech to and around the fetus or infant have significance for the developing sense of self? Eimas, Siqueland, Judezyk, and Vigerito (1971) ask a related question: Why is it that the human child masters language without the formal training that will later be needed to learn reading or arithmetic? As early as 5 months, infants can recognize their name, and by 7 months can identify to whom "Mommy" and "Daddy" refers. Eimas et al. conclude that the infant must have an innate capacity to process and categorize the basic elements of speech, such as, for example, prevoiced and delayed voice onset time, positions of stops in articulation, categories of vowels, and pitch contours.

A charming illustration of the infant's ability to associate pitch contours and rhythms as a neonate and young infant is found in a study by DeCasper and Fifer (1980). Babies were read to from *The Cat in the Hat* by their pregnant mothers during the six-and-a-half weeks before birth. Tested after birth, neonates sucked to hear their mother's voice reading the book they had heard but not a different Dr. Seuss book. Thus, even before birth, infants form an implicit memory of heard speech sounds. Further, neonates a few days old will suck on a pacifier to hear the sound of spoken syllables but not of nonspeech sounds (Vouloumanos & Welker, 2007). Brazelton (1980) reported that 10-day-olds turn their head preferentially to their mother's voice rather than their father's or another woman's.

Kuhl and Meltzoff (1982) demonstrated that infants 18 to 20 weeks old coordinate speech and vision. The infants were shown two juxtaposed filmed images of a woman's face articulating, in synchrony, two different vowel sounds with consonants "pop" and "peep." When the sound track presented one or the other of the sounds, 73.6% of infants looked longer at the face that matched the sound. If, unlike ordinary speech, only the vowels were presented, matching decreased.

Some of the infants responded to the auditory stimulus by producing sounds that mimicked the adult female. As in conversational games with their parents, the infants took turns, alternating their imitations with the speech of the woman on the screen.

Thus far we have emphasized the manner in which neonates and infants create phonetic categories from the acoustics of speech. To our description of the infant as bathed in the sound of human speech, we now add that the infant is also washed in the sounds of music – the music of the human voice speaking and, especially, speaking with a baby. And we return to our question addressing how infants master language without formal training by responding that words are packaged with music. Some speech sounds make up the "music" of the surround, sometimes pleasant and cheerful, sometimes angry, sad, or fearful. Some speech is directed to and with the infant as conversation – "music" with prosody (Knoblauch, 2000).

As Panksepp (2008) claims, "Musical affective prosody engages the communicative effort of infants more than any imaginable cognitive-propositional thought" (pp. 47–48). And as Woodhead (2010) adds, the melody of speech "forms a musical prosodic bridge to the infant's right cerebral hemisphere language development" (p. 52). Parents the world over follow the same essential pattern in talking to infants, a pattern as tuned to an infant's receptive capacities as any design could make it. Parental prattle, often called "motherese," is characterized by syntactic simplicity, segmentation, a slow tempo, a limited repertoire of highly repetitive, expressive melodic patterns enhanced by pitch variations using endings with an overall rise. While the speech patterns of parent-infant conversations are universally similar, the language used is not, and over the course of time that makes a difference. Before 10 to 12 months infants anywhere in the world can respond to and categorize any phonemes used in human speech (but not sounds that are formed synthetically). After a year of age, however, infants no longer respond to spoken sounds they have not heard in the common usage of their environment. The restrictive categorization of their "native" phonemes has a more profound impact on the developing sense of self than simply a language learning capacity. Languages in both the nuances of their phonetic structure and their prosody convey and build cultural and socioeconomic affiliation. Verbal and prosody patterns often are responded to in terms of "he's one of us" or "he's one of them" with profound implications for intimacy or tribal distrust and exclusion. Recall George Bernard Shaw's *Pygmalion*, or its delightful reworking as *My Fair Lady*. Eliza Doolittle is not only taught to rebuild her speech, but the rebuilding of her speech eventually transforms her entire sociocultural way of being. Eliza emerges a "different" person – that is, she experiences a major shift of personhood.

10 What is the significance of the bidirectional mode of infant-caregiver interplay and the inferences and attributions that emerge?

The studies we have presented so far have predominantly documented intrapsychic contributions to an infant's agentic sense of self. As such they understate the contributions of parents and the rich complexity of the interplay. The question above takes us more squarely to the interplay between caregiver and infant, and to dyads' unique contributions as the two exchange back and forth looks, gestures, and sounds. The sense of self in the form of a "nascent personhood" is created in the mind of a mother as she infers the infant's intentions and goals. The mother assigns attributions to the infant. Infants create their own story as they use specific body movements that in turn define the experience of self with other for both themselves and their mother. The mother's capacity to process her exchanges with her baby and to construct workable expectations of the meaning of these exchanges has profound implications for attachment security and for the sense of safety enjoyed by the developing experiential self.

Starting with the premise that maternal care requires an accurate interpretation of an infant's cues, De Castro, Ayala, and Mayes (2010) studied positive and negative attributions that 323 mothers made about their baby's intentions. These attributions ranged from positive: "I feel my baby likes to be close to me" and "I feel that my baby makes eye contact in order to encourage me to play"; to negative: "I feel that my baby does things that bother me just to be mean" and "I feel that my baby does not appreciate what I do for him" (De Castro et al., 2010, p. 547). The authors found that negative attributions predominated in a small group of younger mothers with moderate to higher levels of depression. In this study, positive attributions, when they occurred, were explained by two factors – intention to communicate and intention to please. The majority of mothers rated the babies as having a mid-level intention to communicate. Depressed mothers by contrast gave excessively high or low ratings to intention to communicate. The authors suggest that attributions of excessively high levels of intentions to please might represent a pathological tendency to idealization.

In general, that mothers attribute intentions to their babies implies that the mothers regard their babies as having minds, desires, feelings, intentions, and goals that are similar to theirs. For mothers to regard their babies as having intentional minds that interact closely with theirs is quintessential for meaningful secure attachment.

34 The First Year of Life

Further, a mother telling her baby "Oh, you are hungry and want me to feed you, not play with you now" facilitates language development and especially "intimate" language based on each having a feel for what is in the mind of the other.

We emphasize again that infants are bathed in the words and music, the music of human speech. Many verbal communications utilize the music to convey values that regulate the doer's doing, indicating what actions or feelings are good or bad. Many communications convey judgments about the value of the infants themselves: "She is the best baby; I love her so" or "He cries and won't stop; he is driving me crazy." Caregivers form these attributions by combining more or less accurate perceptions with unconscious fantasies and biases. Indeed, each neonate enters the world with a certain history already created in the imagistic representations of parents, siblings, and other family members. These conscious and unconscious preconceptions and expectations may be modified by or remain impervious to actual encounters with the infant. Whether modified or unchanged, they are made explicit in attributions that seem to pop up spontaneously in the dialogic flow of families. When the attribution is felt to fit it is easier to adopt. When the attribution is not felt to fit or is devaluing it must either be repudiated at some cost or accepted, leading to the experience of a "false self" created by pathological accommodation (Brandschaft, Doctors, & Sorter, 2010).

In treatment, past attributions, by others and by the patient's own self, appear as identity themes and influence personhood – as strongly evidenced in the case of Mrs. H. Current implicit or explicit attributions, by the patient about the analyst, and attributions made or implied by the analyst about the patient, are often core features of transference and countertransference. The approach we (Lichtenberg, Lachmann, & Fosshage, 1996) describe as "wearing the attribution" is central to exploring the meaning of these emergent attributions.

What does an analyst "wearing an attribution" mean? A patient tells his analyst, "You sounded cranky yesterday." Or he says, "When I talk about my father's superior attitude, I wonder about you." Rather than assuming the attribution of crankiness or superiority is a projection of the patient's feeling and/or a transference from a past figure or relationship, the therapist opens her reflection to picture herself in the attributed attitude, feeling, or relational configuration. She may find herself fully or partially as represented. If so she can recognize the intersubjective context in which the feeling or attitude is activated. Even if she can't find herself there, her openness to self-examination, to reflectively considering and discussing the issue with the patient provides a model for their mutually productive exploration and an ambiance of fairness and honesty. In childhood and later relationships, as in treatment, mutual reflection about attributions enhances the enlivening of the self.

A Tale of Two Babies

A baby's and a caregiver's body movements are significant bidirectional contributions to early communication (body language) – that is, to the interplay between the agentic self and the caregiver. Frank and LaBarre (2011) describe six fundamental movements: yielding, pushing, reaching, grasping, pulling, and releasing. These movements are pronounced in the activity of babies. The patterns of these movements are present throughout life as both actions and as metaphors for embodied language and thought – an integral component of personhood. In dyads, qualities of these movements operating bidirectionally influence the ambiance that is created between the pair. A smooth, fluid reaching movement by a parent invites a smooth yielding by a baby and a pleasant ambiance between them. Pulling harshly by a child invites pushing away or an abrupt release by a parent and an aversive ambiance between them. The bidirectional challenge that patterns of movement pose to each member of the mother-infant dyad is illustrated in the early development of Cora and Peggy. Each baby was adopted within a few days after birth, three years apart, by the same parents. Cora, when held for feeding, conversational play, diapering, bathing, carrying, or being put to sleep, yielded fluidly into either parent's grasp. Her reaching or pushing away movements were soft, making it easy for her parents to respond with coordinated complementary movements and to establish a pleasant intimate ambiance between baby and each parent.

Peggy, rather than yielding when held for a feeding, squirmed, wriggled, and pushed away even when hungry making it very difficult for her mother to coordinate holding Peggy and the bottle. The parents quickly found that the father's tighter, more muscular grip helped Peggy to settle and yield, making it easier for him to feed and tend her. Both parents were challenged to establish and maintain a positive ambiance between Peggy and themselves.

Cora responded to the inevitable disruptions of care with a capacity for self-soothing, sucking two fingers, gently rocking, and clinging to her blanket. Peggy rocked vigorously, cried loudly, and frequently resorted to head banging. Unlike Cora, who rapidly accepted the comfort of being held, Peggy was frequently aversive to touch. Unlike Cora, Peggy also did not reach to be held in an inviting manner.

For each child the bidirectional adjustments parents and child made to each other allowed the dyad to go on being. But we infer that the affective agentic sense of proto-self and core sense of self differed for each infant. We infer that the imagery of Cora's agentic sense of self and sense of self with other included

36 The First Year of Life

maps or scenes of her living in her skin and body with comfort and confidence. In contrast, we infer that experiential traces of Peggy's finding it difficult, whether alone or with others, to settle into comfort led her to develop a sense of self with reduced confidence. She was left with experiential traces of a lack of confidence that her agency or the agency of others would effectively reduce the distress she experienced as she struggled to live in her skin and body. Similar variance would apply to Mrs. H and her twin. We know that Mrs. H's lack of confidence in her body and her tense depressive outlook brought her into treatment, and we can infer that her easier and more favored twin, like Cora, experienced less distress and a more positive general orientation.

11 How does being a socially competent doer emerge in infancy?

In a far-reaching series of studies (see Beebe & Lachmann, 2002), Beebe and her colleagues have demonstrated the social competence of infants during the third and fourth month. Any social exchange combines patterns of interactive-regulation and self-regulation with other. Baby and mother bring to each exchange the prior regulatory patterns that affect the nature of the ongoing interaction they then co-construct. The research studied detailed observations of gaze, facial expression, vocal rhythm, spatial orientation, and touch. From the observations of these modes of social exchange, inferences were drawn about the cocreation of interactive and self-regulation, the impact of mild to severe patterns of disruption and repair, and the organizing effect of heightened affective moments. From our current perspective, we may ask: "How does each of these social interactions affect the agentic sense of self?" We propose that maps of existing categories of self as doer in prior social interactions will be added to, or recategorized, in response to a confirmation or a violation of expectations that derives from the preceding live experiences.

For example, each social interaction that involves maternal speech provides an opportunity for an infant to learn. In turn, this affects the agentic sense of self. Infants learn the emotional climate of their attachment, which is then reflected in their sense of the safety of their doings or as Winnicott (1953) put it their spontaneous gesture. From the semantic content they learn verbal connectors to their smiles, frowns, and movements, as well as presumed intentions and goals. "The mother verbalizes the source of agency when she remarks '*You* did it!' or 'Oops! *I* dropped the cup!'" (Vivona, 2011, personal communication). Along with guides to the source of agency, caregivers' verbal and affective comments include statements of values about the doings of either or both: Don't bite; don't pull on mother's ear or glasses; don't soil; don't throw food; don't touch yourself there. Or, I'm sorry; I got the soap in your eye; I love you when you smile at me; Oh, I forgot to bring your blanky to bed. Many examples of parental speech are about who is doing what to whom and a value evaluation about the doing. All of this, naturally, is also being conveyed by the music of speech. The result, we believe, is that the early images (or schemas or maps) of the agentic self include a valence of nonconscious value judgments that influence further agency and the later formation of more abstracted values, morals, and ethics.

In another study Beebe and colleagues (2010) took on the challenge of predicting attachment classifications at 12 months from a microanalysis of a 4-month mother-infant face-to-face communication. The research evaluated modalities of attention, affect, touch, and spatial orientation. The attachment literature has argued that the mother's sensitivity is the principal factor determining secure or insecure attachment. In the current study, Beebe et al. give a nuanced, balanced view. They examine the ways in which infant and mother's communicative activity is contingent on the responses of the other (mutual regulation). They also examined one form of self-regulation for both infant and mother – that is, the ways in which the infant's communicative activity was consistent with (predictable from) his prior communicative pattern, and the ways in which the mother's was consistent with (predictable from) her prior communicative pattern. Using this lens, we argue that predictability becomes a major factor in agency along with the more apparent coordination of intent based on explicit cues. The experience that dyadic interactions are predictable over time bolsters the sense that the actions of each and together are intended – that is, are an expression of agency. Beebe and her colleagues further note that predictability can be observed either in a midrange, or in a high or low range. A high range of vocalization coordination was particularly predictive of future C (resistant) or D (disorganized) attachment at 1 year, and a low range predicted an avoidant (A) attachment style.

Typically, in discussions of the contingency involved in mother-infant conversation, emphasis is ordinarily placed on bidirectionality – that is, the extent to which what each person does is predictable from (not caused by) the doing of the other. Commonly less emphasis is given to the significance of how each one – mother and infant – develops an implicit capacity to predict his or her *own* behavior in a particular repeated context. We believe that infants' learning to predict how they will act and interact (do and respond) in familiar contexts is a core experience leading to a sense of self-knowledge and self-confidence. Prediction

38 The First Year of Life

in our usage is not exact but probabilistic, context sensitive, and flexible. The capacity to predict both the doings and response of others and of *oneself* expands from the early infant-caregiver interchanges to interactions and contexts throughout life and is a prerequisite capacity for establishing and utilizing a therapeutic relationship.

12 What is the infant's experience of being a playful doer doing in response to the invitations that come from the nonhuman environment: a ball is to throw, a teddy is to hug?

It has been jokingly said that success in life can be measured by the "toys" a person has acquired. Personhood commonly includes much that relates to the inanimate world – cars, boats, jewelry, cell phone, apps, and computers. Winnicott (1953) long ago recognized the infant's use of blankets and cuddlies as transitional ground between the toddler's sense of self and the affectionate caregiver. Here we present more detailed evidence based on the discovery of a group of mirror neurons that *respond to objects and to the actions they invite.*

Experiencing the self as an enlivened agent gets a boost from the properties of objects in an infant's surroundings. Animate objects (people and pets) and inanimate ones (toys and cuddlies) in the environment offer particular opportunities for actions. The repetition of these actions creates neuron networks that promote both actual and virtual manipulation of the objects. Adenzito, Adezatom, and Garbarini (2006) describe the discovery (Rizzolatti et al., 2004) of two distinct groups of neurons in the premotor cortex that fire when specific actions are executed:

> The two neuron groups differ in the sense that, even if there is no *active* execution of a given action, one neuron group is activated by the mere *observation* of an object towards which the action may be directed. The other neuron group is activated by observing another person executing that action with the object.
>
> (Adenzito, Adezatom, & Garbarini, 2006, p. 748, italics original)

The authors argue that both neuron types are bimodal with respect to motor and perceptual input in that each fires when either executing a motor program or simply recognizing an action or an object that would be involved in a motor program:

> When an object is under observation, a motor schema appropriate to that object is activated (e.g. for shape, size and spatial orientation) *as if* the observer were interacting with it. Similarly, when observing another individual exerting an

action with an object, the observer's neural system is activated *as if* he himself were executing the same action.

(Adenzito, Adezatom, & Garbarini, 2006, p. 749, italics original)

These findings suggest that infants form meaningful intentions and goals via a pathway that is largely independent of physiological needs and interpersonal triggering. These findings thus suggest two distinct pathways to a child cuddling her teddy. She may feel lonely and rummage among the soft toys in her crib and find her teddy and cuddle it – using the remembered image from prior iterations. Or in crawling around her room, she may come upon her teddy and respond to the appeal of its potential for cuddling. In this instance, the intention and goal emerge spontaneously as the observation of the object activates interest and joy and associated memories while the neuronal network images the play activity. In a sense Toys "R" Us is not only is a catchy name for a store but is also touches on the sense that both our body and our attachment figures "'R' Us." The perceptual and motor activities of toys, body, and people live, develop, and thrive as images highly receptive to nonconscious and conscious activation via subsymbolic, imagistic symbolic, and verbal symbolic processing. The subsymbolic rapid processing of the intention to throw a ball whether by anticipated plan or spontaneously on sight of the ball sets the pattern for the universal human (and nonhuman) love affair verging on addiction for toys and games. The captivating power of throwing the ball includes the inherent inclination to learn to correct for error and improve skill by the nonconscious reviewing of a mistake (Arnetoli, 2002). The bimodel motor and perceptual activation triggered by inviting objects combines interest, joy, curiosity, puzzling, and problem solving with efficacy, pride, competence, and confidence. These are the emotional experiences that propel the intentions and goals of the exploratory/assertive motivational system. The basic pattern of human response to inviting objects is not governed by an explicit rule but is an emergent property of neural networks that self-organize over time.

Our playing with others, and with others even though we are alone, is an important component of our addiction to playing with toys. Modeling actions from doing with the other while observing the other doing is an important emergent capacity in itself, but not as important as the development of playfulness as a quality of the doing. Parents play with babies and babies play with parents. Each sticks his or her tongue out and the other responds. Each smiles and giggles and the other responds. Parents play tickle games, hide-and-seek ("I *see* you"), and "gotcha," as well as grab at the baby or toss him or her in the air. Parents hand babies toys or get their babies' interest using music makers and pull toys. Why? To share joy,

40   The First Year of Life

to stir up excitement – basically to enliven the individual and joint sense of self. Play is learning, learning to be a doer doing and learning how to live enjoyably, learning to seek that enjoyment, that playful spirit, when playing with an actual other or when playing alone. So, is an infant alone when playing on her own with a toy? Stern (1985) comments:

> If a six-month-old, when alone, encounters a rattle and manages to grasp it and shake it enough so it makes a sound, the initial pleasure may quickly become extreme delight and exuberance, expressed in smiling, vocalizing, and general body wriggling. The extreme delight and exuberance is not only the result of successful mastery, which may account for the initial pleasure, but also the historical result of similar past moments in the presence of a delight- and exuberance-enhancing (regulating) other. It is partially a social response, but in this instance it occurs in a nonsocial situation.
>
> (p. 133)

Consequently, whether with another or alone with an appealing inanimate object, play derives in large part from an infant's experience with human inter-subjective shared doing and joyous emotion. Stern notes that the infant's evoked companion when playing alone is not the imagined or fantasied playmate of a later age but an activated memory of a specific instance of joint play and "the shared and mutually induced delight about the successful mastery" (Stern, 1985, p. 133). This portrayal of play ties together significant experiences derived from the enlivening quality of attachment intimacy, the exploratory joy of mastery, and the pleasure of successful mutual interactive regulation of developing physical skills. Throughout life, the ability to activate playing together with others in actuality or when playing when alone and yet not feeling lonely is the foundation for friendship, creative learning (playing with ideas), and successful wooing and sexual compatibility. In therapy, moments of playfulness, of humor and wit, are often precursors of positive change.

13 How do infants acquire the ability to be a doer who can both *initiate* interactions with others and *cooperate* with the initiatives of others?

Here we consider the significance for the agentic self of the evolution-based capacity for cooperation. The initiation of action by the infant and interest by the mother and vice versa – more properly, the bidirectionality of emergent intentions – leads to positive expectations. Using the framework of Kohut's (1971) definition of the self as a center for initiative, bidirectional cooperation establishes a cohesive, confident experience of self.

An infant's spontaneous initiating and cooperating with the initiating of others are essential features of an infant's forming an adaptive agentic sense of self. Recall Ann and the birth of her daughter, Katie. Katie, now at 6 months, and her mother are observed in a feeding episode in a home video. Katie sits in a feeding table. Ann is opposite holding a spoon filled with a gooey cereal mix. Katie's father is making the video. Katie holds her arms up at her sides, freeing her mouth for entry while her fingers are actively opening and closing, mirroring her mouth. Throughout Katie is verbalizing. Her mother speaks occasionally – "Isn't that *good*?" At times her father hums along with Katie's vocalizing. As the tape begins, Katie opens her mouth in coordination with Ann's offering a spoonful; the excess food surrounds Katie's mouth. After the spoonful, Katie drops her arms, moves to rub her gooey mouth area, and begins to look around – first at her father and then in general. Ann waits while Katie explores. Then, poised to continue feeding, Ann advances the spoon as Katie looks at her with her arms up at her sides again. At this moment, Katie begins to vocalize and Ann waits and then feeds. At the next spoonful, Katie, seemingly ready, moves her hands to her mouth as the spoon arrives getting the mix on her hands. Ann cheerfully exclaims: "That was a finger shot." As the face load grows, Ann wipes Katie's mouth and Katie's smile changes to an "I don't like it" frown. Gradually Katie's interest in the feeding lessens, and the intervals lengthen slightly. Then father begins to talk to Ann, who looks at him as they banter. Katie's gaze, face, and head droop and her body slumps. This shift to an aversive state lasts only a few seconds as Ann refocuses her attention on Katie. As Ann moves her head back to address Katie, in synchrony Katie looks up, her arms ready for the next feeding. But before the spoon arrives, Katie drops her arms twice banging rapidly on the table.

This two-minute segment is a microcosm of an infant embedded in a family. Within that holding environment, she is developing her affective agentic sense of self in a balance among cooperation, initiative, and aversion.

Cooperation

Katie has learned to hold her arms to free her mouth, to watch her mother for the approach of the spoon, and open her mouth to take in, chew, and swallow. Ann has learned to watch Katie for signs of readiness and to advance in a rhythm that coordinates with Katie's. Following the midrange model of Beebe and her colleagues

42   The First Year of Life

for a good level of coordination, Katie could predict her own pattern of behavior, Ann hers, and each could predict well enough the responses of the other to adjust to them. Of course they missed once – the "finger shot."

Initiative

For brief periods Katie would look away – sometimes exploring her father, sometimes the room, and sometimes her fingers. Several times Katie seemed more interested in exploring the range of her vocalizations. Each time Ann waited without intrusion or impatience to get the feeding done. Within the feeding, the initiator of each "feed" was difficult to discern – their timing being too dance-like.

Aversion

Two instances of aversion occurred. The first lasted a few seconds as Katie objected to her face being toweled. The second aversive moment would constitute a disruption-repair sequence. Ann and father's banter took attention away from Katie long enough for Katie to become withdrawn – her gaze, face, and head drooped; her body slumped. Katie and Ann's connection was quickly restored with the aversive response continuing in Katie's two bangs on the table, which was ignored by both parents, who retained their genial attitude.

In a paper on the early stages of initiative, Hoffman, Popbla, and Duhalde (1998) studied 239 feeding situations of 41 mother-infant pairs videotaped at home at 30-day intervals from the beginning of spoon feeding at 4 months until 1 year of age. "Initiatives are defined as pre-intentional, non-reflex activity, emotionally charged, and readily influenced by environmental responses. Initiatives emerge in a spontaneous way from the subject acting as agent" (Hoffman et al., 1998, p. 358). The research team chose feeding situations because of the inherent challenge for an infant to initiate on her own despite the risk of confrontation with her mother's intent to complete the feeding and the challenge for the mother to respect her infant's initiative. The findings indicate that a positive maternal response leads to an increase in the number of initiatives, and a decrease in interrupted attempts, aversive reactions, and/or intense conflict. As infants increase in age from 4 months to 1 year, favorable maternal responses increase. From 7 or 8 months onward infant experimental activity and play grow in complexity. The authors distinguish between "aversivity" and "conflictivity." Aversivity is the infant's opposition – keeping her mouth shut, turning her head away, growling, and throwing herself backwards – without the mother's involvement. Conflictivity involves both the mother and the infant in an aversive interaction. A sequence would be as follows: Mother concludes the infant isn't going to eat. She towels the infant's hands and face. The baby's experimentation having been interrupted, she throws a fit. Both scream at each other, banging, and throwing spoons and food in the one case, napkins and bib in the other case. The authors conclude that initiating is an important contribution that infants themselves make to the development of their sense of self.

14 Parallel with the trajectory for those infants developing a secure capacity for bidirectional initiating and cooperating, what are pathways that lead to disruptions of initiation and failures in cooperation?

A tape made for research in a center for teenaged homeless mothers shows a 17-year-old mother with her attractive, nicely dressed 9-month-old daughter, Kierra. Mother and Kierra are sitting on the floor with toys scattered around and between them. Mother hands Kierra a mouthing toy yet within seconds takes it away and replaces it with a cuddly animal. Kierra holds the cuddly animal with interest; in 25 seconds, mother replaces it with the mouthing toy. Kierra takes it, starts to mouth it, stops, and mother begins to play with a push-sound toy, distracting Kierra. At this point, Kierra begins to look away from her mother, trying to ignore her as mother introduces more toys. Finally the mother stands and, holding Kierra, tries to get the 9-month-old infant to walk. Put down again with the toys, Kierra cries loudly and mother says, "You don't want to play no more?" In the next taped sequence at 1 year, Kierra is alone on the floor ignoring the toys and crying. Mother tries to introduce a play phone that Kierra ignores.

This tape provides a defining illustration of the impeding influence of parental intrusion on an infant's development of initiative. In Kierra the foundation of a sense of self as doer doing is obstructed. Kierra is prevented from completing any exploratory initiative. The sequence moves from aborted attempts at aversive withdrawal, and later to tears, but not to conflict. Many of the viewers who have studied the tape find it disturbing. Several have concluded that Kierra's mother's hyperactive, overstimulating behavior results from her misguided motivation to have Kierra succeed at play and to walk prematurely. While her goal may have been positive, she lacked the knowledge and skill needed to reach her goal. She did not have the sensitivity to read Kierra's signals except for the final aversive rejection. This affectively flat though seemingly well-meaning 17-year-old "child" mother could only resort to paralyzing controlling – a trait she had evidenced in earlier caretaking interactions with Kierra since birth.

Children can be controlling, too. Solomon, George, and DeJong (1995) studied children classified as controlling at home and in school at age 6. Sixty-nine middle-class kindergarten children and their mothers were studied using the Ainsworth strange situation separation and reunion; the children also enacted doll-play stories about attachment-related themes. The results demonstrate that children classified as controlling manifest a distinct category of attachment differing from those classified as secure, avoidant, and ambivalent. "The majority of controlling children depicted the self and caregivers as both frightening and unpredictable or frightened and helpless" (Solomon et al., 1995, p. 458). Mothers of controlling 6-year-olds describe themselves as helpless or unable adequately to protect their child. Controlling, then, is a brittle behavioral strategy adopted by the child to cope with fear and helplessness. Eventually that child may become a parent. Kierra's mother gave no evidence of fear per se but did seem to be using a form of controlling hyperactivity to cope with helplessness. Undoubtedly, the mother's early life experiences contributed to her extremely limited sensitivity to her baby's signals as well as to her emotional immaturity and an apparent deep passivity. Given these handicaps Kierra's mother was limited to relying on controlling behavior to try to develop a sense of agency in her child only to have her approach destroy any chance of success. Similarly, to recur to our analytic case, Mrs. H became a controlling child (and adult patient) to deal with both her fear of blunted agency and initiative and her early helplessness in an ever-present competitive situation with her more advanced twin.

The Agentic Self and Mental Processing

In this section, we illustrate core processes that underlie the formation and functioning of motivational systems in relation to the developing self. Lived experience is extremely complex as evidenced by the constant shifts from order to perturbation to tipping points. How does the sense of self and personhood retain cohesion despite the constant shifting of motivational states of diverse affects, intentions, and goals? We examine the capacity to categorize, symbolize, and predict as a basis for organizing the multiplicity of lived experience. These processes beginning in infancy underlie the lived experience of the nonconscious proto-self, the evolving core conscious sense of self, and finally the sense of self experiencing expanded consciousness and full reflective awareness.

15 What are the many processes that lead to the emergence and functioning of motivational systems, and how are motivational systems integrated with the sense of an agentic self?

An infant's ability to form workable predictions is based on the early capacity to form categories. Infants detect differences in features of brightness, shape, patterns, faces, time intervals, odors, sounds, and tastes. They evidence preferences in features and, from brief exposures, generate rules that govern their expectations. A series of studies, referenced by Beebe and Lachmann (2002), demonstrate how adept babies are at translating information about features from one perceptual mode to another. A category is formed as an infant perceives regularities and forms a prototype from these regularities.

Our proposal of motivational systems is based on the premise that, from fetal life to death, human experience is categorized in groupings of related affects, intentions, and goals. Categorizing involves recognizing both the similarities – the essential features – and the distinctions. In other writings (Lichtenberg, Lachmann, & Fosshage, 1989, 2011) we have described the features that characterize the similarities and distinctions between first five and now seven motivational systems: regulation of physiological requirements, attachment, affiliation, caregiving, exploration and assertion of preferences, aversive antagonism and withdrawal, and sensual/sexual. The images, scenes, or maps of each system form early in infancy and undergo continuous categorization and recategorization throughout life. As systems, the criteria of categories are not fixed; each motivational system functions between order and flexibility (chaos), and has moments of overlap with the functioning of other systems. Some affects are core features of one system but can be experienced in any system. For example, interest is the primary activator of the exploratory system but can be and often is active in other motivational systems. Safety and affirmation are central to the attachment system but play a role in other systems as well. Complex indeed! But this is only a portion of the complexity, since for each system, categories based on experience form at three levels, as Wilma Bucci (2002) has proposed. Before proceeding more directly with our question then, we need to take in some of the complexity obtaining to categorization.

Bucci's (2002) multiple code theory provides a description of three systems by which information (experience) is processed. The three systems, the subsymbolic, symbolic nonverbal, and symbolic verbal, are connected by a referential process that links "all types of nonverbal representations to one another and to words. *Emotional schemas* – the psychic structures with which we are centrally concerned – are made up of components of all three systems" (p. 768, italics original). However, the initial core of the emotion schema is built on subsymbolic sensory, somatic, and motoric representations.

The subsymbolic system is the least appreciated in traditional psychoanalytic theory. Its correlates include emotion as a nonconscious physiological experience, procedural memory, primary process, intuition, "listening with the third ear" (Reik, 1949), signal anxiety, nonconscious emotional communication (telepathy), and motor actions that had been regarded as reflexive. While grounded in emotional schemas, the subsymbolic system has the capacity to organize nonconscious systematic forms of thought by making computations about common actions and bodily functions. In all experience, including the functioning of motivational systems, subsymbolic processes hum in the background.

Subsymbolic processing occurs as "variation on continuous dimensions, rather than generated through combining discrete elements as in symbolic forms" (p. 769) of words or discrete images. As development goes forward, subsymbolic processing develops in complexity and scope. In this connection, Bucci cites such evolving subsymbolic dimensions of the sensory modality as "the feeling of the wind, the taste of a wine, the overtones of music" (Bucci, 2002, p. 769).

Paralleling Bucci's emphasis on basic emotional schemas, we suggest that in the motivational system for the regulation of physiological requirements, subsymbolic processing describes the affective registry of variations in the continuous sensations of body systems – the hum of living in one's body. When the attachment motivational system is active, subsymbolic processing refers to the affective registry of variations in the continuous sense of safety and being mirrored – the hum of intimacy as it applies to the sense of self. And, moreover in attachment, subsymbolic processing refers to the affective registry of variations in the continuous sense of the ambiance created *between* the members of the dyad – the hum of intersubjectivity. When the exploratory system is active, subsymbolic processing registers the affective variations in the continuous flow of interest and efficacy – the hum of feeling invested. When aversiveness is an extended experience, subsymbolic processing describes the affective registry of variations in the continuous state of irritability, anxiety, sadness, envy, shame, or humiliation – the hum of negativity. When sensuality is an extended experience, subsymbolic processing registers the affective variations in the continuous flow of pleasurable sensation – the humming and buzzing of an aroused state.

Subsymbolic processing differs from nonverbal (imagistic) and verbal symbolic processing in its reliance on the immediacy of parallel distributed processing rather than on more deliberate sequential processing. We will return to this issue below. For now, to clarify, *sub* does not refer to a less significant or less complex means of information processing, but indicates a means that underlies the nonverbal (imagistic) and verbal processing. While grounded in the experience of affect (activation of the limbic system), subsymbolic processing of information serves as a nonconscious guidance system for many situations of decision-making about the exercise of agency. "Subsymbolic 'computations' underlie hundreds of common actions from recognizing a familiar voice to entering a lane of traffic, and account as well for complex skills in athletics, and for creative work in sciences and the arts" (Bucci, 2002, pp. 769–770).

Addressing functions comparable to what Bucci refers to as subsymbolic computations, Stuss (1992) describes comparator functions capable of discriminating between discrepant experiences in a way relevant to motivational systems. The lowest level compares sensory perceptual input with expectations created from prior experiences of affective agency. The operations of the lowest comparator level are virtually automatic and nonconscious and facilitate daily ongoing behavior of a repetitive nature.

While Stuss emphasizes the more cognitive aspect of subsymbolic processing, Lane (2008) takes up the emotional aspect. Lane refers to primary emotion – the phylogenetically older behavioral and physiological expression of an emotional response. This level of processing provides successful adaptation to immediate environmental challenges, and the physiological adjustments needed to meet the challenges. "The time saved by having behavior directed by implicit processes could potentially mean the difference between life and death in life-threatening situations" (Lane, 2008, p. 221). Primary emotion contributes to nonconscious background feelings and bodily states that color conscious experience, and to inference and decision-making.

Bucci, Stuss, and Lane all regard the subsymbolic level as entailing nonlinear parallel processing that begins as the neonate's mode of responding to stimuli. Through subsymbolic and imagistic symbolic processing neonates rapidly organize experience emotionally into behavioral patterns. When verbal symbolic processing comes on line, the earlier modes of here-and-now processing remain, taking on new complexity throughout life. Bucci notes similarities between the subsymbolic processing level and Damasio's concept of a nonconscious proto-self based on neural maps representing ongoing aspects of the body. In a way consonant with Panksepp's and our concepts, the agentic origins of self in Damasio's understanding of the proto-self involve feelings and emotions that facilitate alertness to problems and a well-organized set of responses directed to immediate action solutions to the problem.

48 The First Year of Life

The research and theories we have summarized here lead to a reconception of unconscious processing that substantially expands Freud's dynamic unconscious (Fosshage, 2011). Experience and consciousness are not synonymous (cf. Donnel Stern's "unformulated experience," 1997; Stolorow and Atwood's "prereflective unconscious," 1992; and Daniel Stern et al.'s "implicit relational knowing," 1998). Consciousness is not a *sine qua non* of experience. As Panksepp's work suggests, experience, an essential feature of the functioning of the proto-self, can be recognized when the limbic system is activated and the organism (fetus, neonate, or adult) as a whole is affected. Being affected, we believe, is demonstrated in the agency (and sense of an agentic self) that results both from initiating actions and being a receiver. Using the example of the neonate sucking to hear her mother read *The Cat in the Hat*, the proto-self experience in that case is demonstrated in a parallel-process immediate response based on a set of expectations formed from the experience of the prior reading. We speak of agency as both doing in the sense of taking in, being a responder to the auditory stimulus, and doing in the sense of sucking to activate the reading. Self as agent is both receptor and actor. The subsymbolic nonconscious processing involves activation of the limbic system and a comparator function – this reading of *The Cat in the Hat* is like, is an analog of, the prior reading of the story, while the reading of another Seuss story is not. And an immediate behavior, the sucking to hear the voice, indicates that the entire organism is affected. The same process occurs when an adult recognizes a familiar voice or, at a much more complex level of computation, enters a lane of traffic, to use Bucci's examples. Thus we add adaptive nonconscious experience to the dynamic unconscious or to the nonverbal imagistic and verbal symbolic systems.

Let us pause for an interim summary of a few points. A proto-self precedes the sense of a core self. Nonconscious processing of information precedes core consciousness and extended consciousness. Subsymbolic and imagistic symbolic processing precedes verbal symbolic processing. The nonconscious subsymbolic proto-self takes in and simultaneously processes motor, visceral, and sensory experience forming images, maps, or schemas based on neural networks involving reentry. (In contrast, symbolic processing combines discrete elements of imagery, metaphor, and language.) We emphasize that "precedes" does not mean "is superseded by." Each mode of processing and each manner of experiencing self and consciousness persist and develop further as time goes on.

Back to our question. As children proceed through the first year into the second year, the emergent core self creates imaged accounts of others, the effect of their own processing on themselves, and the relationship between self and others. Their awareness of their feelings facilitates their planning of new responses specific to

The First Year of Life 49

the immediate problem situation (Damasio, 1999). And the capacity to give focal attention to one's own background feelings also develops (Lane, 2008).

It is this basic set of responses upon which motivational systems are built. Stuss describes a second-level comparator function that facilitates selection of responses that give conscious direction to the pursuit of a goal. Anticipation, play, goals, attentional focus, and self-monitoring are coordinated consciously. Unlike the rapid, almost automatic, nonconscious first-level comparator functioning, the second-level comparator feedback is slow, deliberate, and effortful. A third-level comparator, also slow and deliberate, integrates input from the first and second levels with more complex aspects of self-awareness, self-reflection, and mentalization.

The buildup of language continues the transformation from proto-self and sub-symbolic and imagistic symbolic processing to an agentic sense of self in which the earlier modes are integrated with (but not replaced by) verbal symbolic processing. The buildup of language tends to be continuous. Infants begin with the subsymbolic categorizing of phonemes, pausing rhythms, and intonations and the basic dialogic patterns of communication. Infants and then toddlers move to single-word designators for familiar people, objects, and self, and then to grammatical sentences.

The nonverbal and verbal systems affect each other through referential links that develop in caregiver-infant interactions:

> The making of a referential connection requires joining the multichanneled, parallel and analogic contents of the nonverbal schemata, which are often private and unique to an individual's life, to the discrete, sequential, and logically organized verbal modality, which is the shared communicative code.
>
> (Bucci, 1997, p. 7)

Bucci proposes both a verbal symbolic system and a nonverbal system comprised of images (imagistic symbolic processing [Fosshage, 1983; Paivio, 1971]). The images can enter directly into consciousness, be assembled in dreams, or be connected to and serve as a link to verbal forms. In adaptive functioning, the subsymbolic, nonverbal, and verbal symbolic systems are connected through referential links. Solano (2010) comments:

> For example, an emotion experienced subsymbolically may find representation in images and words. Failure of formation or subsequent interruption of

these connections between the subsymbolic (implicit) memory of a traumatic situation and symbolic systems leaves behind a "nameless" subsymbolic activation, which may find spurious symbolic connections, so giving rise to mental symptoms such as phobias or delusions. Or it may find no symbolic connection and disturb the functioning of an organ or apparatus. This disturbance may range from the functional level (irritable bowel, premature heart beat) to the more severe organic pathologies [in interaction with genetic vulnerability].

(pp. 1454–1455)

Linking between systems that process experiential input is clearly a major factor in the functioning of self-agency. Linking can be temporarily bypassed when quick survival decisions require momentary dissociation. In these occurrences the referential system remains flexible and capable of easy restoration. In unresolved trauma, avoidant dissociation (delinking) persists and new information is actively blocked.

16 What allows the agentic self to advance from the early modes of intentions and goals to the greater complexity of the verbal symbolic system and creativity?

Thus far we have emphasized the impact of a doer doing and of affect on the formation and experience of self. In tackling our new question, we investigate affect and action in a different way, by describing the significance of metaphoric processes across the entire spectrum of subsymbolic and imagistic and verbal systems. Metaphoric processes transfer cognitive and emotional meanings via the recognition of implicit and explicit similarities and dissimilarities of lived experience. The richness of the sense of self and personhood could not develop without the contribution of metaphoric processes to human imagination and creativity.

The search for meaning, coherence, cohesion, intimacy, sexual fulfillment, a secure base, and a multiplicity of other intentions, including a capacity for work and play, all entail goals attributed to humans and to a healthy sense of self. Recognizing similarities and differences and transferring meaning across a domain of similarities are capacities required for the achievement of any and all of these goals. Modell (2009) has designated the capacity to recognize similarities and differences and to transfer meaning as metaphoric processes. In contrast to the more usual definition of metaphor as a reference to subtle and often unexpected dualities of verbal meanings, as exemplified in poetry and the writing style of authors like Henry James, in development metaphoric processes are defined in terms of their ability to create and influence meaning across the entire spectrum of subsymbolic and imagistic and verbal process levels.

For Modell, a cognitive capacity for metaphoric thought may have evolved in humans before the acquisition of language and conceptual metaphor. Metaphoric thought enables the creation of images that involve the seeking of similarity and difference. As we have seen, seeking and recognizing similarities is embedded in the process of categorization that is responsible for the creation and organizing of motivational systems and the sense of self. Seeking and recognizing similarities may also be an important process in Bucci's referential links between subsymbolic and symbolic systems. Modell's point is that unconscious "memory of the self and its intentions is constantly recontextualized, and the link between conscious experience and unconscious memory is provided by metaphor" (Modell, 2006, p. 25).

Reviewing references to intentionality, Modell states: "Meaning is achieved through *action* in the world, and in turn, the self is altered by that action" (p. 19, italics original). To this he adds that "the self changes itself as a result of what it has encountered as a consequence of its actions" (p. 19). In these passages Modell emphasizes, as do we, the unconscious aspect of the formation and transformations of the sense of self as agent. Agency, the doer doing in the world, is integrally related to the sense of self, subsymbolic and symbolic processes, and metaphor. As well as in language, metaphor exists "in gestures, visual images, feelings, and bodily sensations" (p. 27). Multimodal in its sensory connections, metaphor accesses both unconscious and conscious memory. Modell defines metaphor "as *a mapping or transfer of meaning between dissimilar domains (from a source to a target domain)*. Metaphor not only *transfers* meaning between different domains, but by means of novel recombinations, metaphor can *transform* meaning and generate new perceptions. Imagination could not exist without this recombinatory metaphoric process" (2006, p. 27, italics original).

Modell cites "balance" as a prime exemplar of the spread of metaphor via similarity and the transfer of meaning. Beginning with the upright toddler's shaky sense of balance, the physiological state experience links with imagery derived from tottering objects to seesaws to metaphoric word usage about falling in love and losing one's balance. "The organizing schema of balance is mapped onto diverse and totally unrelated domains, such as the visual arts, music, jurisprudence, intellectual reasoning, and mental health" (2006, p. 77). Balance in these instances resides not in the domain itself but represents an attribution derived from the metaphoric linking. Another example is the recognition by sculptors such as Giacometti and Caro that a vertical sculpture no matter how abstract will

52 The First Year of Life

invariably elicit an association to the human form. In response they began to produce horizontal pieces that when placed on the floor or table activated an observer to walk around them. The observer is "made" into a doer and "forced" to view the sculpture through a different metaphoric schema.

Trauma degrades the metaphoric process in that past meanings are linked to the present without transformation. The present is conflated with the past, imagination is constricted, ambiguity is lost, and the "customary play of similarity and difference" (Modell, 2006, p. 39) is absent.

17 When the doer doing encounters obstacles, how do we understand the divergent pathways leading toward confidence and optimism or alternatively toward insecurity and pessimism?

The doer doing inevitably encounters obstacles that disrupt the doer's intentions to initiate or take in, to act or respond. Disruptions can arise in situations in which the doing is in interactions with others, or involves the doer's own body, or engages the inanimate world. Ordinarily, in the face of disruption, through the resources of infant and caregiver, the connections that have been breached can be restored, intentions and goals can be reactivated, and the negative effect on the infant and mother's mental state can be repaired. Which is to say that disruptions are most often followed by repair in the familiar disruption-repair sequence identified in both the developmental and treatment literatures. To disruption and repair, however, we add the crucial idea of restoration in the sense of restoring the empathic bond that existed previously. We believe the frequency and ubiquity of experiences of disruption-repair and of restoration of the empathic relationship has a profound cumulative effect on the emergence and maintenance of confidence and optimism or devitalization and pessimism. The cumulative effect of how disruptions play out, and of the success or failure of restoration, can profoundly influence the tenor of expectations of the developing sense of an infant's agentic self in one or more motivational systems and later in the tenor of personhood.

Lived experiences of having intentions and mental states disrupted, and having expectations violated, are so frequent that their overall effect on the sense of self is difficult to specify. At one extreme are traumatic events – an infant's loss of a caregiver (a severe disruption to the attachment motivational system), a hospitalization for an illness (a disjunction affecting physiological regulation and the sense of bodily integrity), violence and abuse in the home (an intense accentuation of aversive responses). At the other end of this continuum are patterns of matching, brief mismatching, and rapidly restored matching. Here we find experiences of joyful, surprising violations of expectations such as the "I'm gonna getcha" game. Match-mismatch-rematch patterns have been tested in experiments on visual, auditory, and tactile coordination in rhythms of dialogue (Jaffe, Beebe, Feldstein, Crown, & Jasnow, 2001). These patterns occur repeatedly in every infant-caregiver conversation – for example, during feeding, diapering, play, putting to sleep, awakening, and dressing.

However, in a well-functioning "facilitating environment" close observation reveals a surprising degree of variability in coordination between caretaker and child. Infants and mothers have exactly matching facial expressions or a shared focus of attention when playing together about only one-third of the time (Malatesta & Haviland, 1983; Tronick & Cohn, 1989). Yet, Tronick and Cohn (1989) have also found that when well-attuned infant-and-mother pairs enter an unmatched state, 70% of the dyads returned to a match within two seconds.

How does a return to match come about? A neonate's capacity to return to a calm state after stress is evaluated in The Brazelton Neonatal Assessment Scale (1973). After a stress is introduced, the time needed by the infant to dampen aversive arousal is measured. The test also assesses the help required for neonates to stabilize their state and reengage. The capacity for infants to self-regulate after stress, referred to as resilience or self-righting, can also be observed prebirth (Brazelton, 1992). The fetus responds to dystonic stimuli by a dampened arousal state, even sleep, and then returns to a normal arousal when the stimuli become more moderate.

Infants thus bring into an engagement with a caregiver a greater or lesser capacity for resilience in response to disruption as can be seen in Cora and Peggy and in the more developed twin and Mrs. H. A limited capacity for resilient response to a disjunction can be observed in babies born premature like Mrs. H, and in infants whose mothers used addictive drugs. Meanwhile, caregivers bring their sensitivity or limitation to bear in creating or responding to a disjunction. In the Jaffe et al. (2001) study of vocal rhythm coordination, mothers classified at both extremes – those who were the highest and lowest in coordination with their infant – contributed to the most problematic outcomes. Hypervigilant intrusive tracking offers an infant no opportunity to devise a strategy for being a doer – that is, no space for being an initiator of an intention. Accordingly, consistent with common-sense expectations, the highest degree of rhythm coordination was predictive of disorganized attachment. However, the opposite is no better: When mothers typically failed to coordinate rhythms and monitor disruptions, infants were left to their own limited resources. This was predictive of avoidant attachment. Midrange coordination by contrast gives infant and mother, like Katie and Ann, the necessary play space to

54   The First Year of Life

develop strategies for dealing with match-mismatch-match experiences. Midrange coordination provides the dyad with more room for initiative, testing, and exploring possibilities and is predictive of secure attachment. Midrange coordination improves the opportunity for the infant not only to predict the caregiver's actions and intention but also to anticipate the infant's own actions and implicit intentions. The bidirectional ability of infant and caregiver to predict both her own intentions and those of the other enhances their coordination and cooperation as evidenced in the Ann and Katie spoon-feeding sequence. The same ability for coordinated implicit prediction of intentions facilitates repair after a disruption.

In this context, we may note that three of the best known experimental designs for assessing infants, The Brazelton Neonatal Assessment Scale, which we have discussed, Tronick's still-face situation, and Ainsworth's Strange Situation, all study stress (disruption) and its aftermath (restoration and repair). In the still-face experiment (Tronick, Als, Adamson, Wise, & Brazelton, 1978) the mother violates the infant's expectation of a continuation of an ongoing conversational interaction by presenting a still, unsmiling face. Infants then attempt to elicit the expected interaction by their smiles and gestures. When the infant gets no response from the mother, the infant looks at the mother with an animated face but then turns away. After repeated failure, infants withdraw and slump with head and body averted from mother. With the mother's return to a smiling interaction, a period of variable length ensues in which each contributes to reestablishing contingent responses and a positive state. Eventually, the connection is restored and the infant's aversive state is repaired. Four-to-six-month-old infants who in their ordinary interactions with their mother have generally experienced successful repairs have more adaptive coping skills. They will continue to signal their readiness, shift their focus to explore, and use self-comforting touch. Infants who have had little success in ordinary interchanges have poorer coping skills, arch away, slump, and enter a disorganized state. Coping styles stabilize and by 1 year are predictive of secure or insecure attachment.

In the Strange Situation, the stress is created by having the mother unexpectedly leave the testing room where she had been playing with her 1-year-old infant. Reacting to the loss of a secure base, a securely attached infant evidences distress. The infant runs to the mother on her return, is picked up, held, and comforted. Mother and infant work together to restore contacts and a state open to reactivating play.

The adapted coping skills of securely attached mother-infant pairs to the mother's leaving the play room are well stabilized by 1 year. Less adaptive stabilized coping skills are evidenced by insecurely attached 1-year-olds. Some infants

The First Year of Life   55

evidence distress on the mother's leaving, seek reconnection on her return, but then pull away and resist comfort. Other insecurely attached infants evidence no distress, divert their attention, and avoid reconnection. Still other infants, in the disorganized (D) category, lack any workable strategy, start toward their mother only to fall, be distracted, or appear dissociated.

We suggest that from innumerable instances of match-mismatch-match 1-year-old infants have derived an implicit message that has an impact on their future sense of an agentic self. One message might be the following: When I face a loss, a stress, a disruption, I along with my mother, or my mother along with me, or both together, can manage to restore our connections and a positive affective state. I can expect that, in conjunction with the help I need, my intentions and goals can play out toward effective and satisfying outcomes. This could apply to the disruption-repair and restoration experiences of Peggy and her mother, and of Katie and Ann in the feeding episode.

Or, alternatively, when I face a disjunction, I cannot expect that I and someone I look to for help can manage to achieve an effective and satisfying outcome. Rather I fear and expect that I will end up in a contentious seeking and pulling away, offering and resisting, with a disappointing other. This might apply to Cora.

Or, when I face an obstacle I need to handle my fears and the challenge to my goal on my own. I distrust and avoid helpers, expecting them to be indifferent to my intentions, and to reject my appeals and protests. This could apply to Kierra and her mother.

Or, when I am confronted with a situation that arouses intense aversive feelings, I can't find any strategy I can rely on. My intentions become confused and I will seek or fall into a dissociative state.

The still-face and Strange Situation assessments are experimental designs that provide experiences analogous to the repeated instances of disruption-repair and restoration of everyday life. A fundamental precept of self psychology is the importance of sequences of disruption and repair in analysis. In the course of every well-established empathically based analysis, the ongoing exchange will be disrupted by the analysand's experience of a failure in empathy by the analyst and the activation of an aversive response. Separately or together analyst and analysand will recognize the source of the disruption, repair the breach in their communication, and restore their intersubjective connection. These disruption-repair and restoration experiences provide opportunities for highly productive exploration. Each successful repair enhances the confidence of each participant as a doer doing with the other.

Winnicott (1941) describes an experimental design in which 5- to 13-month-old infants are placed in a set situation that activates uncertainty and anxiety. The baby

56 The First Year of Life

is positioned on her mother's lap so that she can reach for an attractive mouthing spatula. The mother is instructed to attend to Winnicott and not interfere with the baby. The baby puts her hand to the spatula, hesitates, and looks at Winnicott and her mother with big eyes. She may wait with her body still, withdraw, or bury her head in her mother's blouse. Gradually she becomes brave enough to let her feelings develop, heralded by a change inside the mouth as saliva flows. Before long she puts the spatula in her mouth with a general freeing of body movement. Winnicott regards the transition from anxiety and hesitation to daring to act on desire as a valuable increase in self-confidence. Now the baby regards the spatula as belonging to her. She bangs it on the table and then drops it introducing a "you pick up, I drop," game. Winnicott views the moment of hesitation and the ability or inability of the baby to take the next step as what he calls self-expression and we call agency, and this is seen as an indication of mother-baby interplay in the home. Harrison and Tronick (2011) state: "Perhaps the most revolutionary concept in the paper is Winnicott's description of the small repetitive events that underscore the developmental and, correspondingly, the therapeutic process" (p. 977). Parallel to our view that an infant's step-by-step experience of success in being a doer doing with others builds a confident sense of self, Winnicott (1941) states that "little steps in the solution of the central problems come in the every-day life of the infant and young child, and every time the problem is solved something is added to the child's general stability and the foundation of emotional development is strengthened" (p. 245).

18 How do we understand early memory that interlocks with subsymbolic and imagistic symbolic processing and influences the trajectory for the doer's varied expectations, intentions, and goals?

Throughout this chapter we have made numerous references to memory. We began with a reference to Katie as a neonate quieting as she heard Ann's familiar heartbeat. We noted the experiment of the infant who sucked to activate the reading of *The Cat in the Hat*, which she had heard read while in utero. We described the reciprocal memory-based prediction that contributed to the cooperation in the spoon-feeding episode of Ann and Katie. We noted a mother's repeated failure to recognize her daughter's initiatives leading to the memory and expectation of disruption and paralyzing negativity. We described our assumption that Mrs. H's symptom of her open mouth being unable to close was a body memory of feedings in which the nipple was lodged in her throat. The infants who averted from "the hinderer" and looked at and reached for "the helper" at 3 and 5 months remembered and distinguished between the two episodes.

The First Year of Life   57

Memory in all these instances from the subsymbolic and imagistic symbolic period differs from the experience of storage and recall that adults identify as remembering. Rather memory in these cases is an integral component of patterns and maps that emerge from the doer doing with others and with self that, once formed, have dispositional influence. The brain does not store memories,

> it stores traces of information that are later used to create memories. As a consequence it rarely, if ever, expresses a complete veridical picture of past experienced reality. A complex neural network, involving many parts of the brain, acts to encode, store and retrieve the information, which can be used to create "memories."
>
> (Fonagy, 1991, p. 606)

We propose that "been there, done that, experienced that, am predisposed to do it and experience it again" is the organizing principle for the creating of implicit memories.

In the classic memory experiment of Rovee-Collier, Sullivan, Ehright, Lucas, and Fagen (1980) an infant was placed in a setting in which a ribbon tied to the baby's ankle was connected to a mobile. The baby learned that kicking her feet moved the mobile. Placed in the same setting 24 hours later infants of 2 or 3 months kick their feet to move the mobile. The "been there" is the setting imagistically recognized as a familiar context. The "done that" is "kicked and made the mobile move." The experience of "done that" is the pleasure of efficacy. The "predisposed to do it again" is to reexperience the affect of interest, the power of agency, and the pleasure of a visual display that the baby has brought about. The combination of been there, done that, experienced that, am predisposed to do it again provides the origin of the intentions and goals of the exploratory/assertive motivational system: a context that invites exploration, the activation of interest, the pursuit of efficacy and competence, and the assertion of preferences for pleasurable sensations.

Variations of this experiment described by Beebe and Lachmann (2002) reveal the subtlety of early implicit memory. The mobile the babies kicked on the second occasion was altered from having 10 items to having 2 (Singer & Fagen, 1992). Half the babies cried. The babies who did not cry remembered for up to three weeks that their kick moved the mobile. The infants who cried did not kick to move the mobile. An initial assumption was that the negative affect interfered with memory. However, when three weeks later the infants who cried were shown the mobile in motion, they began to kick. Beebe and Lachmann (2002) report: "The researchers concluded that the problem for these babies was not the storage of memory but its retrieval. The heightened negative affect at the moment of learning interfered with access to the memory" (p. 72). We view it differently. In our view, ordinary moderate affect, unlike traumatic affect, does not interfere with cognition. A change in ordinary moderate affect in the same setting creates a *new* memory. The disruption of expectation in the babies who cried created a different map – a different been there, done that, experienced that (cried) that affected the predisposition to do it again. Instead of interest and working toward a sense of efficacy (activation of the exploratory/assertive motivational system), the affect was negative. The breach of expectation experienced by the infants who cried activated avoidance, a shift from the exploratory system to the aversive system. The cueing reminder when the infants saw the mobile in motion then facilitated a switch in intentions. Now the infants shifted from aversion to exploration. Seeing the remembered visual image reactivated the remembered pattern and its affective rewards.

These experiments are about much more than 2- and 3-month-old infants' sensory, motor, and memory capacities. The experiments are about the emergence of lived experience in the here-and-now. Lived experience emerges from processes that integrate the coordinated activation of the perception, cognition, affect, and memory systems. The lived experience of self doing and the environment in which the doing occurs consists of a context, an effective intention, and a goal. Thought of this way, there are no implicit memories as such; there are only experience-based maps that integrate memory and potential retrieval with the other foundational systems (perception, cognition, affect, and recursive awareness). The mapping and categorizing of lived experience influences the processes that lead to each emergence of intentions and goals and the accompanying sense of self-agency. Fosshage (2011) addressed the wide scope of capacities and intentions of implicit memory: "Implicit processing includes a number of memory systems – skill learning, priming, classical conditioning, modeling, and procedural learning" (p. 59) as well as implicit relational knowing.

We return to the example of the baby and mother in Tronick's description of the "mood in the morning." It provides examples of the many facets of implicit memory. The episode begins with the mutual recognition of faces and the expectations of a greeting response – the foundation of an attachment reunion experience. The implicit memory of the greeting response affects greetings and reunions throughout life. In Tronick's example, a shift of emotion ensues, beginning with the mother's negative state, then moves to her rallying when she sees the effect on the baby, and ends with a return of negativity that persists for the baby. The

The First Year of Life   59

following five factors that Tronick identifies as accounting for the baby's persisting negative morning mood illuminate aspects of implicit memory.

First, affective waves alter the threshold of their activation based on affective input. Negative emotional experiences set the amplitude of the negative wave at a heightened level close to the threshold. Small negative activations have a strong impact; positive activation then requires a greater activation to reach a threshold. This hypothesis integrates experience (affective input) with process (affective activation waves). The registry of implicit memory shifts depending on the *threshold level* that is needed for activation (retrieval).

Second, affect states recruit and augment affect triggers. The baby's negative response to her mother's disappointing negativity recruited the baby's pinched facial expression, clenched fist, body tension, and autonomic system arousal. To this picture would be added implicit memories of similar experiences. Implicit memory resides in body states that self-organize in response to an affect trigger – an embodied memory.

Third, mutual augmentation results from the effect of mother's and baby's negative emotion on each other. Implicit memory arises from and is critical for the powerful effect of transactional affective interplay. The role of implicit memory in mutual affective regulation or dysregulation places implicit memory in a central position in the early attachment search for security, and continues to be significant throughout life.

Fourth, recurrence of the negative experience increases the impact of all the factors. Psychoanalysis has long attempted unsuccessfully to explain via explicit verbal processing the impact and compulsive nature of maladaptive patterns repeating. We see connectionist theory as offering a better alternative. Just as Tronick's wave activation theory places "memory" of moods in the level of threshold for affect activation, connectionist theory places memory in the strength or weakness of neural connections and the activation of experiential/ behavioral patterns. Taken together we hypothesize that connectionist theory places repetition of experience in the very fiber of developing neural networks (Rumelhart, McClelland, & the PDP Research Group, 1986). Information processing is accomplished through the simultaneous activity of a network of simple processing elements. Connections between units become stronger in response to repetitions of a particular interaction. Knowledge is built into the system by virtue of the strength or weakness of connections. Expectations of a negative mood in the morning that influence the mother-baby interactions are regarded as patterns of reactivations of negative affective units that have developed strong

60 The First Year of Life

connections between them due to repetition. The sense of self is now consciously influenced by the strength or weakness of the neural networks that activate affect and agency.

Fifth, regulation via the biological clock fixes the repeated affect into a temporal pattern. Implicit memory includes aspects of the context in which repeated lived experiences occur. Retrieval may be triggered by any element of the context – the setting, a sensory experience (Proust's Madeline), or a temporal link like morning or an anniversary reaction.

Taken together an implicit memory involves the following:

1 a threshold level for affective activation,
2 an embodied memory,
3 the influence of mutual affective regulation,
4 the strength of neural connections, and
5 the context in which repeated lived experiences occur.

Implicit memory is required for an infant to form a sense of an agentic self and to function as an effective doer doing. Personhood cannot emerge without the ability to have a discriminating reflective view of generalized aspects of self and others and to have explicit autobiographic memories of self with others – past, present, and future. We have centered our presentation on the early developments that contribute to the emergence of an agentic sense of self and the capacity to organize and categorize affects, intentions, and goals. In 1989, Lichtenberg took up Stern's (1985) question: Is the infant capable of remembering the experience of agency, coherence, and affect? Both authors agree that a motor memory, a perceptual memory, and an affect memory occur as integrated units, what Stern (1985) called "a small but coherent chunk of lived experience" (p. 45). Through repetition the infant gains enough experience with the separate major self-invariants (agency, coherence, and affectivity). Also through repetition, as the integrating processes reflected in episodic memory advance "the infant will make a quantum leap and create an organizing subjective perspective that can be called a sense of a core self" (Stern, 1985, p. 99). And Lichtenberg (1989) says:

A psychoanalytic theory of adaptive and maladaptive motivational functioning is about lived experience throughout life. Lived experience is about how we human beings consciously and unconsciously seek to fulfill our needs

The First Year of Life   61

and desires by searching in potential events for effects that signal for us that experiential fulfillment.

(p. 2)

We believe we have illustrated the many experiences and processes that confirm and flesh out these early hypotheses of Stern and Lichtenberg.

Does it matter if analysts recognize that neonates and infants have a "mind"? The existence of an infant's mind would be irrelevant to analysts who regard early infancy as an autistic or undifferentiated stage. The experiences and processing of a subsymbolic and imagistic symbolic period would not qualify as a mind at play for analysts who define mind as coincident with fully expanded consciousness, explicit memory and recall, and language-based symbolic process. As developmentalists, we believe every aspect of life will be influenced by what preceded and each new experience will influence what comes after. Each aspect of the early life developments that we have described influences later experiences and processing. The influence of any one experience on later development will be variable. Sometimes the influence on later development will be predictable, often not. Sometimes the origin of an influencing prior experience can be traced, often not. Because of the importance we ascribe to them in clinical work, we highlight thresholds for the activation of affects, forming and being the recipient of attributions, and success or failure in managing disruption/repair and restoration episodes. In addition to their clinical significance, we view these experiences and processes of infancy as threads that influence the experience of self and personhood throughout life. While we have focused on the emergence of these threads in early parent-infant relationships, they are relevant throughout each stage of life. The initial patterns may be reinforced, modified, or transformed through subsequent lived experience in every epoch as well as in a psychotherapeutic relationship.

19 What role do experiences of awe and admiration play in the doer's evaluation of others and self?

Special heightened affective moments of early (and later) lived experience emerge from an action by a caregiver and/or an infant that elicits a positive surprise, a feeling of awe, and a positive appreciation (admiration) of the doer and the doing.

One-year-old Timmy sitting on the floor next to his mother sitting in a chair was playing with a pull toy that had holes in it to put pegs into. Each time Timmy tried to get a peg in the hole the toy moved just enough to throw his aim off. Seeing his dilemma his mother reached down to hold the toy steady and gently guided Timmy's arm. After successfully placing the peg in the hole, Timmy looked up at his mother, his eyes widened, and his mouth made an O-shape in an expression of awe and admiration. It was as if he were saying: "You are wonderful. You knew just what I needed."

Midge, an active crawler, had for some time tried to walk but each time after a step or two quickly abandoned the effort. One day Midge was busily crawling across the room from where her mother was setting a table. When she glanced over to Midge, mother was surprised to see "her baby" on her feet walking over to her. With a look of delighted surprise she said, "Wow! Look at you! This is awesome. *My baby* is walking. Wait till I tell your father."

Brian, aged 7, was shy and eye avoidant with strangers and even with many well-known adults. Yet, he had also discovered a way of relating through triggering awe with magic tricks and remarkable gymnastic skills.

We believe that experiencing awe and admiration create magic moments in a dyad. In a parent-child dyad in infancy or a patient-therapist dyad, either member may be the activator or recipient of awe and admiration. In a therapy session these affectively heightened moments of meeting, often described as "aha" experiences, add to the confidence and trust of the process.

Reflections on the Origins of the Agentic Self and Treatment

In the course of our prior discussions, we have reviewed many facets of research and observations of the development and lived experiences of infants. From these many perspectives, we have abstracted a series of adaptive capacities and qualities of a doer doing. These capacities facilitate the emergence of an enlivened sense of self prepared to respond to subsequent life changes and challenges. To the extent that these capacities and qualities of a doer doing have become "a good enough" adaptation, they make an exploratory therapy possible. To the extent that these capacities are underdeveloped or maladaptive, they present hazards to treatment and become a necessary focus of therapeutic inquiry. Therapeutic change is inextricably entwined with development. To understand what is being changed requires appreciation of prior (especially early) development. The change itself is developmental and what emerges from the change influences further development.

20 What lived experiences crucial for development in the first years of life are basic to the processes that subsequently facilitate therapy?

The sense of self, whether cohesive or fragmented, enlivened or deadened, emerges from infants experiencing themselves as a doer doing – acting and responding with others and self. The presence or absence of mutual receptivity in early relational experiences sets a dispositional tone for being a doer with others including as a patient in a therapeutic dyad. In tackling the above question, we will identify 12 trends emergent in early lived experience that influence the success of therapeutic action. These capacities and dispositions can facilitate therapeutic change, but at times they can also constitute the specific capacities that have to undergo further development for change to occur.

Balancing the Thresholds for the Activation of Positive and Negative Affective Experience

The potential for the initial activation of any specific affect or mood depends on the combined interplay of innate genetic factors, conditions in the intrauterine environment, and the neonate's and infant's lived experiences. For the activation of a specific emotion in any moment of time, a balance is set by the lived experience that emerges from the interplay of the infant's proclivities (vulnerabilities and/or resilience) and the influence of individuals in the developing child's environment. A parent's happy smiles elicit the smiles of an infant open to respond and an eager readiness on both their parts sets the stage for the next exchange of joy. Conversely an infant with a depressed mother will be pulled in by her mood state, and she by his negative responsiveness, and both by the emergent negative ambiance they cocreate. With each subsequent life event, the threshold level for the activation of a positive or negative affect may be reinforced or modified. In everyday life and in treatment sessions, good experiences – conscious and/or nonconscious – will reinforce a prior low threshold for positive emotions or, if repeated, gradually modify a higher threshold, lowering it so positive emotion can be more readily experienced. The opposite is also true. That is, positive experiences can raise the threshold for negative emotions so that they are less readily experienced. Clinically, we recognize how readily some patients respond to even mild stimuli for fear, anger, depression, guilt, shame, humiliation, and embarrassment. We can think of working through as operating at an implicit level by which repeated affective exchanges during sessions gradually raise the threshold for

64 The First Year of Life

activating negative emotions and lower the threshold for activating positive emotions. These gradual changes in affective receptivity will register nonconsciously in the ongoing lived experience of the patient in and out of the treatment. Especially important for the therapeutic relationship is the implicit cumulative effect on the developing ambiance in the dyad and the facilitation of the emergence of new more positive experiences.

Having Explicit and Implicit Confidence That Disruptions in Relationships and Pursuits Will Be Repaired and a More Optimal Context Restored

Repetitive experiences of caregiver-infant success or failure in repairing disruptions and restoring an optimal context for each to be a doer with the other establishes an implicit expectation that upsets can be mastered with confidence – or a fear and dread that they can't. Failure to respond to a child's physical or severe emotional distress, especially if prolonged or repetitive, erodes confidence in the effectiveness of the reparative effort of others and also of the child. Treatment, by the very nature of dyadic or group relationships, inevitably provides instances of new and old experiences of disruption in communication and in empathic understanding as well as opportunities for restoration of positive connections and confidence. Each current disruption experience during analysis stands on its own as to its trigger but also carries a trace of the implicit effect of the success or failure of early and recent attempts to repair the emotional damage and restore a safe attachment.

Having a Sense That Oneself and Others Have a Positive Identity Based on Affirming Attributions

Parents continuously form attributions about their children and about themselves as parents, often beginning even before the children are born. As soon as their capacity for verbal symbolism emerges, infants give word labels (good boy, good mommy, bad boy, mean mommy) to their prior and current imagistically encoded experiences. An attribution may be limited to how oneself and others are seen to be in specific areas of endeavor, or it may become a more generalized identity characterization of the self and the other. Cumulative attributions from past and current lived experience enter treatment in the form of implicit or explicit expectations and identity characterizations of the analysand with the analyst, and of the analyst with the analysand. (The expectation and characterization of many aspects of the analyst with analysand we call transference.) Whether specific or generalized, attributions in infancy and analysis emerge in a context. The relational context of analysis points to the need to recognize the analyst's contribution to the emergence of the patient's attributions about himself and the patient's attributions (transference) about the analyst. To bring the analyst more fully into the lived experience of the analysis we (Lichtenberg, Lachmann, & Fosshage, 1996) have described a way for the analyst to "wear the attribution." In comparison with a more traditional interpretive approach to transference, an analyst's openness to "wear the attribution" provides the patient and therapist with a more complete opportunity to explore the old, recognize the present, and form new ways to view self and others. Some attributions about self and others including the therapist may become more or less concretized and appear in therapy as difficult-to-dislodge fixed-identity themes.

Having a Sense of Being Known and Fully Recognized for One's Authentic Qualities, Capacities, and Sensibilities

Closely tied to the power of attributions derived from prior lived experience is the child's (or patient's) sense of being known. When a child has been mirrored across a range of affects, intentions, and goals and especially modes of responsive relating, the child can place herself more securely in the world with what Winnicott called a true self. Frequently the child's own deep sense of authenticity exerts a positive influence on the responses of others to her. Alternatively when the child's inherent emergent capacities have been ignored, rejected, or misidentified, the child is often forced to adopt a false self via pathological accommodation. Analysts like parents often have to distinguish between agreement and compliance, and to recognize when an objection reflects antagonism or self-assertion on the part of each with the other. Then, too, in the therapeutic dyad, recognition of each party's authentic positive and negative qualities, abilities, and sensibilities is critical for therapy to progress.

Having the Ability to Predict One's Own Reactions as well as That of Others

An infant's capacity to predict her patterns of initiation and response can be observed in proto-conversations and then in a widening range of intentions and interactions. A child's full sense of knowing himself can only be achieved if, as he develops, he is able to integrate his initiatives and responses with those of others – an integrated dual contingency. In therapy, a patient's sense of being known arises from a match between the therapist's empathic attunement and the patient's self-knowledge. For the sense of being known to emerge, patient and therapist must be able to predict implicitly their own intentions and goals and those of the other. A factor often understated in treatment that mirrors the caregiver-infant relationship is the importance of the analyst being able to predict when and how she can influence her patient. And possibly more significant still is the analysand's learning that she can predict when and how she can have an impact on the analyst.

Forming and Sharing Narratives

From the continuous flow of body sensations and perceptual input, while awake, drowsing, or asleep, and no matter whether the individual is task focused, meditating, or engaged in mind wandering, beginning with imagistic symbolism in infancy the human mind forms narratives – at first imagistic sequences, then scripts, and later verbal depictions. Narratives are essential organizers of experience and the emergence of developmental experiences adds complexity to narrative capacity. Metaphoric links emerge between each of the narrative forms. Narratives are essential for an autobiographic sense of self based on temporality – that is, past, present, and future. We might say that to be human is to create stories, dramatizing them in a theater of the mind, and then to live more or less comfortably in the stories we create – about ourselves, others, and ourselves with others, and the world we live in.

The capacity for empathy is intimately linked to sensing into stories. In analysis, crucial narratives appear as "model scenes" (Lichtenberg, 2005; Lichtenberg et al., 1996) derived from the patient's past experiences as well as events the patient and analyst have shared. Their jointly shared exploration reveals the who, what, where, and when, the full tonal quality of affect, and the implications of moral and ethical values that are implicit in the stories. While narratives and related actions are generally concordant, conflicted patients' doing and narrative are disparate. Then analysts are faced with shifting focus from the narrative to discover an enactment.

Learning, Understanding, and Internalizing Social Norms

Learning, understanding, and internalizing social norms are an early form of adaptation required for children to become social beings. At 3 months infants form narratives centering on moral and ethical values, and by 3 years they appreciate and enforce rules of games. Knowing social norms enhances the doer doing's sense of being able to predict the intentions of self and others and provides confidence in "being in the world." In contrast, when the social "norm" for an infant is to be raised in a family in which abuse regularly occurs or in a neighborhood that is lawless and centered on drugs and violence, the child and later adult's "norm" will test the resources of any treatment situation. When the infant's world is troubled in less destructive ways, therapy itself presents a new field of social norms and a means to explore the patient's adaptive or maladaptive reactions to social expectations.

Sharing Moments of Enlivened Lived Experience

Sharing moments of enlivened experience, momentary or extended, produces a sense of commonality and safety. From the mirror-neuron activation of shared moments of mother and baby extruding their tongues to the shared smile on greeting to the later sharing of humor, an ironic perspective, and aesthetic sensibility – seeing eye-to-eye – invigorates all relationships including the therapeutic dyad. Seeing-eye-to-eye in a treatment is both metaphoric in the use of the couch or telephone and also literal for patients seated or seen on Skype. Does the absence of a direct eye-to-eye connection lessen the opportunity for enriched shared moments, moments of meeting? This question applies especially for patients who as infants had mothers who eye averted, had blank, expressionless facial expressions, or whose most telling shared moments centered on fear, shaming, or sadness as evidenced by research on insecure and disorganizing attachment.

Having the Ability to Play With Others, to Play When Alone and Evoke a Sense of Another, and to Generate a Spirit of Playfulness

A mother playing with her responsive baby, with their eyes widening, tongues extruding, hands moving, brightening at first, then smiling and giggling, breathes life into movement in a shared world of joy and playfulness. The evolutionary preparedness of the newborn is demonstrated by how rapidly, after a mother has initiated a playful interaction, the infant takes further initiative if the mother doesn't. It has been said that play is a serious business and indeed it is. Once well established in the intersubjective realm of the infant in the first year, play provides a foundation, an underlying hum, for many aspects of learning, mastery, sensual and sexual sharing, and creativity. In therapy implicit play with the puzzles of dreams, associations, and the impact of past events helps greatly to lighten the heaviness of the negativity that must be faced.

Experiencing Other and Self Through Physical Touch and Later Metaphoric Touch

Lived experiences involving physical and metaphoric touch help to integrate body and mind. Touch is a significant mode of doing in the development and regulation of a sense of self. Self or caregiver touch provides a means of soothing, of playful arousal, and sets a sensual tonality to doing with both self and other. Self-touch and being touched embody physiological, attachment, caregiving, exploratory, and sensual/sexual experiences. The reciprocity involved in feeling touched emotionally by the other is a fundamental basis of therapeutic intimacy. But what about actual touch – handshakes, sitting close, a consoling pat, a hug – in treatment? Can the result be an activation of an early childhood feeling of deep concern and connection, or is it inevitably a start down "the slippery slope" of seduction? What past experiences of the patient and of the analyst will play out in either the inclusion of touch or its absence, in touch becoming a helpful component of treatment or a destructive influence? The capacities and experiences in this domain begin in infancy, continue to evolve over development, and figure in treatment though how they play out is a matter for exploration on an individual level.

Learning to Cooperate in Spirit and Interaction

Infant and caregiver cooperation is a fundamental basis of reciprocity in all of an infant's doings with others. Cooperation results from the ability of each to recognize and respond to the initiatives of the other, and cannot develop if an infant's initiatives are ignored or overwhelmed. Cooperation involves negotiating the polarities of compliance and opposition. Empathy, sensing the state of mind and intentions of the other, develops in parallel with cooperation. In therapy each experience of cooperation enhances confidence in each person's knowledge of the other, and increasing knowledge of the other and increasing ability to "read" the other's initiatives enhances the ability to cooperate. Children raised in families in which every intention elicits competition conceptualize their own endeavors and those of others as zero sum games of winners and losers, dominators and submitters. Patients with this background regard cooperating as weakness – something only done by "little" people. They filter the analyst's empathic or interpretive effort through a judgment of who is up and who is down.

Experiencing Heightened Affect Moments of Surprise, Awe, and Admiration

A parent's surprise, awe, and admiration in regard to some "wonderful" doing of their infant and an infant's wide-eyed acknowledgement of something "wonderful" their parent has just done facilitate the emergence of a special quality of invigoration that can then be lent to "magic" moments throughout life. A wondrous sunset, a trapeze artist's brilliance, and the "aha" moment of a sudden insight, especially if shared in a therapeutic dyad, are moments in everyday life and in therapy that enliven the human spirit. Alternatively, surprise, awe, and admiration can be exploited by parents, siblings, teachers, and cult leaders or analysts to inspire fear and dread and make them feel powerful and magically brilliant and the child or analysand small, weak, and dependent.

The 12 qualities and capacities for lived experience that emerge in the first year go on to contribute to a momentary and/or overall sense of safety in both daily life and treatment in different ways – and with varying degrees of focal awareness. The capacities for verbal narration and interactive cooperation are in the foreground as explicit aspects of treatment interchanges. Changing thresholds for the activation of affects and moods are implicit influences in the background. Recognizing and exploring attributions, sharing moments of enlivened lived experience, and heightened now moments of surprise, awe, and admiration are fully in awareness. The sense of being known, confidence that disruptions will be repaired, and an appreciation of social norms provide a background hum at the edge of awareness. Affect activation thresholds, many aspects of predicting the reactions of self and others during activities guided by procedural memory, and the processes by which preverbal narrative formation organizes experience are essentially nonconscious. The sensual feeling from being touched physically and psychically, ranging from patterns of tension-reducing self-touch to expressions of metaphoric touch and the felt security of a holding environment, have links across levels of consciousness.

The capacities formed in the first year will be continuously influenced by subsequent lived experiences. Hopefully, with positive experiences, the capacities will mature and their efficacy will become enhanced. Some capacities that had been underdeveloped in the first year may be enriched. Alternatively, later strain or acute trauma and impaired relatedness may limit or disrupt the further development of many capacities.

We have tried to demonstrate that contemporary developmental research has shifted the basis of analytic listening from a focus that highlights conflicts and pathology to a balanced appreciation of adaptive developments that facilitate a sense of safety and a therapeutic relationship. An important consequence for treatment of recognizing the adaptive qualities and capacities that develop very early is that a balanced view helps to facilitate positive change, the strengthening of the adaptive qualities and capacities, and the emergence of new lived experience. The roots of the enlivened self go deep – as, sadly, do the roots of the deadened self – and a treatment that aims at being a shared empathic exploration in depth can only profit by keeping this in mind.

Chapter II

Clinical Guidelines

Therapeutic change is inextricably entwined with development. To enhance developmental processes is central to therapeutic change. To understand what is being changed requires appreciation of prior development and what has subsequently occurred. The sense of self, whether cohesive or fragmented, enlivened or deadened, emerges initially in infants experiencing themselves as a doer doing – acting and responding with others and self. The presence or absence of mutual receptivity in early relational experiences sets a dispositional tone for being a doer with others that subsequent experience either reinforces or changes

In this essay, we apply the 12 psychological developmental processes that we have culled, from the research literature to the treatment situation. These processes, while initiated in the first year of life, continue as central developmental and regulatory processes throughout the life span. Our depictions of the sense of self that emerges from being a doer doing with others and self, and the 12 developmental processes beginning in the first year that enliven the sense of self, provide a grounding for an examination of these processes as they reemerge in therapy. In what follows, we will track these developmental processes as they influence the success of therapeutic action.

When applied to the clinical situation, the 12 qualities and capacities can, in the first instance, serve as an informal checklist. We can ask what the status of each dimension was that characterized the interaction of the patient and the therapist at the beginning of treatment, were the patient and analyst able to negotiate cooperatively the arrangements for starting the therapy? Was the patient strongly reactive affectively to what appeared to be a small negative moment? Was the patient able to experience and react affectively to a positive moment? At the onset was the therapist able to predict comfortably his reaction to the patient's presentation or confused and uncertain about what he was doing and also unable to predict the new patient's responses to him? Did aspects of the interaction point toward a favorable therapeutic process, such as a moment of a shared enlivened experience

72 Clinical Guidelines

or humor or felt mutual understanding? Was there a good flow of narrative communication in terms of words, facial expression, and gesture?

As the therapy unfolds, the 12 qualities and capacities can be used to recognize and evaluate progress in enhancing current adaptive patterns and forming new capacities and undergoing emergent new lived experiences. Has the patient become more resilient in responding to a disruption? Has the therapist become more able to recognize disruptions and better able to discern their source, in terms of both the patient's and his contribution? Do therapist and patient feel increasingly known by each other, especially as each relates to the other in their interactions? Has a new pattern emerged that replaces what had been known with a new, more adaptive authenticity of one or the other or both together as doers doing? Has the dyad been able to engage within a context of a social norm that has become more flexible and enlivened? Does a more favorable old pattern or a newly formed one open patient and therapist to increased experiences of feeling deeply touched? Are there moments of admiration for the sensibility and exploratory skills of one another and both together? Have negative attributions become replaced by new attributions more accurately reflecting the essential strivings of each and of their joint efforts?

As we present a psychoanalytic case study, we address each one of these developmental processes for their relevance in understanding and facilitating therapeutic change. The case was treated by one of us (J. F.), though the discussions of it in the "comments" attached to the narrative reflect our common understanding.

A Wintry Village

I (Fosshage, 1999) have selected an analysand and an analytic process transpiring over a course of 15 years. Over two decades ago, I received a phone call over the weekend from a male analyst colleague; I will call him Jay. I did not know him well. He was a man in his early 60s. In my brief exposure to him, I had experienced him as bright, outspoken, and argumentative. Jay told me that he had fallen in love with an analysand of his. After consulting with his former analyst, he had decided to tell his analysand of his feelings for her and his desire for a social romantic relationship with her, and shortly thereafter, had terminated the treatment. At his invitation she began to live with him – four days after the termination. Three weeks later they agreed that she needed an analyst and I received the call. Recognizing that this was a highly unusual and problematic situation, Jay, implicitly expressing his trust in me, inquired if I would be willing to see her in light of these circumstances. I told him that I would see her and suggested that she call me. He informed me that she was right there and put her on the phone. With a clear voice, she expressed in an enthusiastic and straightforward manner her desire to see me, whereupon we scheduled an appointment.

Several days later, I saw Samantha. Samantha, a woman of 37, spoke well, was quite attractive, dressed in a casual, trendy manner, and demonstrated a charm and outspokenness. Her outspokenness carried a tension that I sensed was part of her battle to overcome squelching influences. Her mood was quite elevated. She was "flying high" and clearly in the thralls of an idealizing love of her now boyfriend and former analyst. I sensed that her elevated mood was not only related to the initial stages of "being in love" that includes a mutually self-enhancing idealization, but also to a somewhat strained, yet valiant effort to overcome anticipated criticism and perhaps also ambivalent feelings of her own. I liked her, felt interested and engaged, and wondered where our work would take us.

Her first treatment experience, she explained, occurred some years back when she was going through marital difficulties and, subsequently, a divorce. She had married in her early 20s and divorced three years later. Her therapist was a "Freudian analyst" who had known her family. She described him as cerebral, unempathic, detached, and unnurturing – warning signals of what I should not be, I thought, that most likely resonated with previous trauma. Experiencing the analyst as too close to her family and too removed to trust, she ended up "manipulating him in orchestrating the session to amuse him and to avoid certain areas." Terminating after two years, she exclaimed to me, "I was fucked by him," for she felt blamed by him and ended up feeling worse.

Approximately 10 years later she sought treatment with Jay. At that time she was feeling profoundly depressed and periodically suicidal. She said that she was conflicted "between what I was bred to be and my inner integral self. . . . My inner self has been squashed and wants out or I will die. . . . I was the perfect child – forget it – I am not the repressed, elegant Swiss-German girl." She had been taught "to control cerebrally" her feelings. As a result, she felt "an Amazon woman in me emerging that was previously smashed." She entered into analysis with Jay on a four- to five-times-a-week basis and began to take Prozac. The analysis lasted for six months.

Comment: (Through these comments we intend to alert the reader to the connections we are making to the status of the 12 capacities and qualities during different periods in the treatment.) In her initial session Samantha was clearly intent on emphatically describing how her parents had not seen or known her "inner integral self" (in our language, *authentic self*). Instead, they had imposed upon her their image of a "repressed, elegant Swiss-German girl." To maintain the attachment and secure affirmation Samantha had to pathologically accommodate (Brandchaft,

74 Clinical Guidelines

1994) her parents' *attributions* and requirements to become "the perfect child"; yet, she was quite aware of an intense defiance – that is, "an Amazon woman" ready to emerge within her.

Based on her report, Samantha quickly became intensely engaged in the work with Jay, fostered by her feeling deeply understood for the first time in her life. With the establishment of an idealizing and mirroring self-object connection, her spirits lifted considerably and medication was discontinued. Clearly the analysis had gone well until the analyst's needs more directly entered the scene. She described how they had become very close, expressing their affection for one another. She recalled hugs at the end of the session, initiated by Jay. His occasional giving her a ride home after a late-night session was somewhat confusing, yet, it was experienced as part of an increasing closeness. Jay, who had been divorced for some time, then told her that he loved her and that he wanted to stop treatment and marry her. She responded positively, for she had never felt so understood and deeply connected to a man. They terminated the analysis and, very shortly thereafter, were engaged to be married.

Samantha and I had connected easily during the first session. Although I was aware of Jay's breach of ethics and the reporting guidelines, I was most concerned about Samantha's welfare. I did not report Jay, for it would have precluded Samantha's analysis. I knew that Jay's analyst was informed and carried the ethical responsibility. My priority was to protect Samantha's analysis. I decided not to express concern to Samantha about what had happened. Samantha was "in love." Any hint of concern could have evoked aversion in her in the service of protecting her loving connection with Jay, foreclosing self-reflection and the expression of other feelings. I overcame my temptations to prejudge the situation by reminding myself that I did not really "know" whether her relationship with Jay might work, as on rare occasions such relationships did. I believe that my openness to this possibility facilitated my listening closely to Samantha's experience and to *her* feelings and assessments – that is, listening from within an empathic perspective.

Comment: In light of what she had already said about a core conflict between her integral self and how she was bred, which left *her authentic self unrecognized*, I was quite aware of not wanting to impose on her yet still another judgment and agenda. In addition, "to know" another person requires understanding from within the other person's perspective (empathic listening), and at the moment she was "in love" despite the problematic context.

Based on her initiative, we decided to meet on a twice-weekly basis, because, in addition to financial limitations, I believe we both felt that she did not want to jump so quickly into yet another intense analytic relationship.

During the next session Samantha spoke about how her older brother had been killed in a car accident over 20 years before. She was the only remaining child. Nevertheless, she focused primarily on her relationship with Jay and how her parents were distressed about him. Samantha described her parents as "cerebral, controlled, intellectual, and scared." Her father had sarcastically quipped, "A patient marries her therapist, every woman's dream!" He saw her as an "invalid daughter" who needed to be taken care of by a man – a powerful disparaging parental attribution. Her mother was also critical and gave Jay what Samantha described as "a manipulative dose" during their first meeting, saying, "You must have a pick of all your patients." Samantha was, unfortunately, all too familiar with these undermining comments in the face of "bad behavior." Shaken by her parents' skepticism, it became even more imperative that she hold steadfast to her love and commitment to Jay.

Over the next six weeks, Samantha spoke about her inner experience, especially using her dreams and imagistic symbolic processing to create a narrative and deal with intense, dramatic conflict. What could not find explicit expression, without jeopardizing her parental connections, her fragile state of mind, and her efforts to regulate herself, erupted in her dream life. The first dream she reported, after four weeks of treatment, was as follows:

I'm an oriental woman; her skin is white, her hair dark, wearing no clothes. The sky is pale – it's very quiet. There's a big dune with white, fine sand. I was at the crescent of the dune to see the ocean – one place I have peace. At the bottom of the dune were two oriental children – small; they were dead. They were laid out on their stomachs facing the ocean. They had died because they had been thrashed on their backs with a huge bouquet of small pink roses. I had also been thrashed on my back.

I repeatedly went up to the crescent of the dune to see. The children changed. One time it was me and my brother – one time, my parents. I'm hurting them in my will to grow.

[She comments outside the dream] I did not intend to hurt others. Sometimes they were my children that I never had. I woke up with my body taut, like there were vultures going to pick my bones.

In our ensuing discussion, Samantha mentioned how, at one point during the previous fall, she was feeling deeply suicidal and developed a welt on her back and had a dream that her mother had put a knife in her back. Here in this dream the pink roses delivered the fatal blows. "Flowers were given in the name of love," she described, "but they persistently killed me, brutalized me, controlled me. They did something so beautiful but deadly." She spoke of two sides of herself: "What I was bred to be and what I am inside . . . I can't bring the two together." For her, to grow, to live from the inside out rather than from the outside in, was tantamount to hurting, even killing her parents. She could find moments of peace fully exposed at the "crescent" of the dune overlooking the ocean, but below her lay the small dead children who had been killed. She ends up terrified of vultures. Retrospectively viewed, these core issues framed much of what was to come.

> Comment: Gradually her life story unfolded during these first few weeks, but in an unusually piecemeal fashion. Her elaborate dreams would often bring up pieces that would then be filled out. While she was highly articulate in person, her waking *narrative* about herself had not yet become all that coherent. It was full of dissociated fragments. Her intense conflict between her own perceptual, affective, cognitive experience – that could serve as a self anchor – and her parents' imperious expectations and wishes interfered with her striving for a more cohesive sense of self. Consumed with these conflicts, and her parents with theirs, Samantha's relational experience had not created the needed space and inner quiet to reflect, nor to form and articulate a more coherent picture of her life. Hence, even the following brief summary could only be constructed over a considerable period of time. I believe that her own narrative had been disrupted by her parent's imposition of their narrative, which was replete with *attributions* that belied her experience and therefore did not take hold.

Samantha's father was highly successful in the arts and her mother was well educated and had worked in publishing. Swiss-German in origin, they raised their family with strong values for education, music, and culture, and for hard work, compunction, and dedication. Rules and regulations were the order of the day. Samantha experienced her mother as often hysterically talking above her and at her. Her mother's quick temper and rages emerged a bit later in treatment. Samantha portrayed her mother and father as tense and busy people who insisted that things were to be done "right." While tension was often in the air and not infrequently expressed overtly, there was little room for reflectively relating emotional experience.

> Comment: In the family, fighting was routine between parents, parent and child, and between children. *Disruptions* were rarely reflectively

talked about and resolved in the family. Instead, self-injuries triggered rage that, in turn, undermined possible *repair*. Similar to their parents, Samantha and her brother, older by four years, fought intensely. Unable to open up the emotional tension to ferret out its meaning, her father finally nailed shut the door that adjoined their two rooms.

Samantha had experienced her family as ricocheted with tensions; yet, she had pride in her family. She was raised to be the perfect model child, the elegant young woman. While success on this front fostered the development of some confidence in her intelligence, attractiveness, and style, she seemed to realize that, in response to her parents' powerful agenda, she had been forced to subjugate much of her own perceptual and affective experience. She continued to wage a terrible battle between "who I was bred to be and who I am inside."

A major tragedy befell her family when her brother was killed in a car accident in his mid-20s. Her parents dealt with the tragedy by shutting down emotionally. They did not talk about her brother. It was as if he had never existed. Soon thereafter, they sold their beloved beach home where, with time, and close to nature, they had lived more fully as a family. The loss of her brother, the further loss of an emotional connection to her parents, and the loss of the valued beach home wreaked emotional havoc in Samantha.

Comment: While Samantha's parents had accomplished and created a cultured family with considerable positive experience, they had great difficulty in dealing with emotional tensions and traumatic losses. At those times, anxiety, tension, and rage dominated the scene (that is, *a low threshold for negative affects* had been established) with scarce resources for reflective processing.

Her dreams, long and complex narratives, were often attempts at desperately trying to deal with these traumatic losses. A small portion of her second dream clearly tells the story:

I am at the age I was then, but also now. We are selling the house. A couple comes to see it. It is very important to me that they are a couple that understand the house. I don't think there is such a couple. D, T (my parents), and I have spent all this time getting the house in shape in order to sell it. All of our hearts are full of grief. Each one of us does not want to give up the house for our own reasons, but we cannot communicate to each other what those reasons are. We are each locked in our own grief and sadness, and led by this pain to pass judgment on ourselves and each other. We stand in judgment on ourselves and assume the rest of the family will also. We proceed to follow the correct "form" of what apparently needs to be done: getting rid of the house that reminds T (mother) of my brother. We follow her lead because she is so unhappy and make the explanation that the house is too big to maintain and therefore must be sold.

Meanwhile, during the first two months of treatment, Samantha's relationship with Jay gradually deteriorated. In contrast to his careful listening and understanding that had occurred in the analytic relationship, she began to experience him as controlling and demanding with little regard for her wishes. She thought of herself as being a very sexual person; yet, she found Jay to be disrespectful and sexually controlling. He reacted to her objections and assertions with rage, which was all too reminiscent of her family. Samantha began to feel that she had given up too much of her life, a feeling that resonated deeply with themes of the past. She had a nightmare in which she was married to Frankenstein – it was Jay. She was trying to escape. In the dream, he and she were both malformed. Not only was this now her experience of Jay, but it reflected how for years she had thought that something was wrong with her. Now, in the ensuing throes of a rapid and unrelenting de-idealization, she began to see Jay as an older, lonely man who was desperately self-focused and controlling. Moreover, he was defensive and unable to reflect or talk about their deteriorating relationship. In turn, Samantha became horrified and ashamed about how she got into this situation. Recalling her analysis with him, she felt that, when she had begun to express her sexual feelings, Jay had encouraged detailed elaboration of them. She realized that at times he had become sexually aroused. Subsequently, he began on occasion to respond with sexual overtones. She had responded in kind, which, now, horrified her. Yet, the ingredients of her response – feeling affirmed, sexual excitement, intimacy, understood, and capitulation – could still not really be assessed. Instead, her distrust and sense of betrayal, rage, and shame became increasingly intense. Within two months she had broken off the relationship against his angry protestations and returned to her apartment.

Her experience of Jay's abusive imposition and betrayal resonated with experiences from her past. Gradually it emerged that her brother had made sexual advances and a trusted neighbor had insistently come on to her when she was an adolescent. Physical abuse occurred with her mother who in rages would strike out at her, slapping her face and "beating the shit out" of her.

Comment: In her relationships with her parents a sense of betrayal in the form of criticism and the imposition of their agendas pervaded. Compliance or defiance that left little space for *cooperation* dominated the scene.

Clinical Guidelines   79

Over the next four months, Samantha felt increasingly angry at Jay's betrayal and manipulation of their trusting analytic relationship. She felt abused and victimized, and harbored deep shame about her involvement. She finally decided to sue him, which for her was an attempt to reassert herself, to impact him, to overcome the sense of victimization, to become a "doer." Her lawyer asked for my participation. In considering the potential repercussions of this with Samantha, not the least of which was the potential for the suit to dominate the analysis, I emphasized the importance of protecting our analytic relationship. I also knew that the analyst in the courtroom is easily discredited as biased, leaving little to be gained by my direct involvement. While I was well aware of the importance for Samantha of my support of the suit, with her agreement, I declined to participate directly in it. Later, she expressed her gratitude. At her lawyer's request I referred Samantha to a psychiatrist who provided a psychiatric evaluation for the suit. After negotiations between the lawyers, Jay threatened violence to her and her attorney. Shortly thereafter, she agreed to a pretrial settlement with financial recompense, which provided some satisfaction along with a sense of retribution.

The experience with Jay had been traumatic and the fallout considerable. Could she really trust an analyst again? Could she trust a man again? She vowed never again to have sexual feelings for her analyst, which was clearly directed at me, for she felt that I, too, would be unable to contain them and would become stimulated and betray her. She felt threatened by an analyst's power as well as by her own seductive capacity. She wrote,

> I cannot accept that I allowed this to happen to me. I cannot understand that I was a victim. I cannot come to terms with my participation in this relationship. . . . I feel violated, ashamed, revolted, helpless, sickened, furious, bereft, betrayed, abandoned, fucked, raped, abused, disgusted. I feel trapped by the trail of abuse and betrayal he has left in me. I feel unclean, unwhole, completely compromised. I cannot accept that I was helpless and powerless to act otherwise at the time.

While her compliance and victimization felt intolerable, her sexual response and active participation were equally unacceptable.

Comment: When distrust was in the foreground in the analytic relationship, I attempted to live in the *attributions* of the transference (Lichtenberg et al., 1996). That is, I attempted to experience her attributions and to understand them in light of whatever triggers might have occurred between us. I understood her attributions to have been cocreated, through my contribution and through her anticipation or construction based on her lived experience in her previous analytic relationship and her parental and familial relationships.

Despite her wariness, Samantha appeared to experience me usually as protective and caring – hallmarks of an idealizing self-object transference – which corresponded with how I felt toward her. She increasingly experienced me as "solid" in a way that helped to reassure her that our relationship would not get out of control, a fundamental prerequisite for our cocreation of new relational experience. During this phase of the analysis, self-object relatedness, for her, was in the foreground, and, for me, my "caretaking" or being concerned with her formed a reciprocal relationship (Fosshage, 1997a). This created a particular kind of closeness, similar to a father with a young daughter, satisfying to both of us. To experience me as a person who would have additional needs, however, was, at this juncture, a powerful trigger of terror. She dreaded that she would again be exposed to betrayal, domination, and abuse. Hence, her experience of me during this time, we learned, needed to be circumscribed around my "caretaking" efforts in order to cocreate the requisite safety and protectiveness.

> Comment: Our consistent reflective processing of *disruptions* that were triggered within the analytic and outside relationships was creating a new procedure for *reparation* (through understanding the triggers and each other's contributions). It was also gradually *lowering the threshold for positive experience* and was deepening a fundamental *cooperative*, trusting connection (that is, trusting that I honored her initiative).

In the work arena Samantha had given up a full-time position with a company in the arts where the corporate structure was oppressive and her particular boss was all-too-intrusive and controlling. She freelanced but struggled financially and suffered from a lack of career direction. She wanted to write but lacked confidence and had not been able to sustain a consistent effort.

In the course of the analytic process that ensued Samantha began to deal with memories and with her affective life that had been frozen off (dissociated). Her dreams, which expressed her imagistic giftedness, were excruciatingly long and painful. As she wrote them, painful memories emerged. I have selected small portions of one dream that occurred approximately 14 months into treatment. The dream opens with Samantha on the beach watching the surfers play in the late afternoon. She must pick up her father and begins to worry that she will be late and be accused of being irresponsible. She writes:

> I am on my way again to my destination. However, I am angry and feel I am "behaving" obstreperously. The surfers have gone, but have left their surfboards behind, standing in tumbles next to the pier. I can see the fish hooks in the sand and the fishing poles beside them. The hooks stick out from the surface of the sand. I sit and look at them first, and then very decidedly walk towards them, all the do's and don't's and restrictions, regulations, controls, musts, have to's, shoulds, always, never to, and will now do's, given to me by my parents are ringing in my ears as I walk across the beach. I want to touch this dark blue surf board; it sits, fin facing me, the underbelly of it slightly worn down, the color rubbed slightly away from being pulled across the sand after being in the water. It's like a blue finned whale. I walk across the fish hooks and feel and hear the hooks puncturing my skin, and curving into it, and out on the other side. I don't care. I must reach out and touch that blue board. I feel the pain of the hooks, but am disembodied from it at the same time.

In her undaunted effort to touch the blue surfboard, she initially finds it necessary to "disembody" herself from the pain of the impaling fishhooks. Later in the dream, she begins to feel the excruciating pain as she tries to free herself from the hooks. She knows that her parents will reprimand her. There is a concert that night, and she realizes that she has ruined their evening for they will need to take her to the hospital to have the hooks extracted. What stood out for us in our discussion was what placed her in jeopardy: her need to touch the blue board and to feel its beauty, despite the exposed fish hooks, and the need to defy her parents' constant admonitions and prohibitions. Her parents would not be sympathetic but would be furious with her, reigniting the desperate struggle to find, in spite of the danger and in defiant reaction against her parent's dictates, some beauty, some freedom, some peace as symbolized in the image of the dark blue surfboard. The blue surfboard was a powerful image for Samantha, capturing her desire for freedom of movement, for gliding with nature, for peaceful existence and beauty, as a way of creating a sense of agency and an enlivened affective experience. It was a solitary experience of enlivenment.

As she wrote out this dream, traumatic memories burst into her awareness – of having been hit by a car and then having been hit by her enraged mother; of being called to dinner, forcing her to leave her cat to die alone; of her broken arm, which

82 Clinical Guidelines

her parents did not immediately take care of; of her not being told the truth before she underwent dental surgery; of her not being told of her brother's death for eight hours after he was killed; and of her father's screaming at her when she saw him naked when she was 11 years old – "the shame he made me feel."

> Comment: Her intention and determination to reach the freedom of the surfboard, "her destination," still required painful, even dangerous, defiance of her parents' agenda. With the lessening of her dissociation, she was able incipiently to feel the pain and to recall the traumatic memories. As long as the pain was completely frozen (dissociated) we had not been able to deal reflectively with the pain and integrate the trauma. If the traumas could be integrated, the *threshold* for the pain of her traumatic memories would be raised.

Close variations of a dream, which had recurred over the previous 14 months, involved her checking her room before she and her parents leave the beach house after the sale. She finds the drawers and closets are full. She writes:

> Everything I own, memories signified by my belongings, tumble, tumble out into my arms. I am always the last. Everyone else is pulled together. They seem, or have denied that they are having any difficulty leaving. This time they are on the ferry line, and I sit overwhelmed in my room finding more and more things to take with me. I have already been chastised for having so many bags. The rest of the house looks like a museum – I just wrote mausoleum. Only my room is chaotic or alive.

We understood that, on the one hand, she was laden with memories that needed to be sorted through and, on the other hand, she was desperately trying to recapture and to hold on to the memories that could provide a sense of stability and self-continuity. But she always felt in a panic in the face of her parents' denial, impatience, and fury. She did not have time or parental help to sort through her belongings one by one, to assess, to reflect, to tarry, to keep them with her or to discard as she desired.

As Samantha dissociated less, her inner world of intense conflict and painful memories emerged more fully, at times becoming excruciatingly terrifying. She experienced powerful urges to jump out her 10th-floor apartment window, which we came to understand was jumping out to "freedom," free of the expectations, the restrictions, the inner turmoil. She became terrified and I became deeply concerned that, at the height of pain, she might impulsively go for this last-ditch effort to end the intense suffering. Medication was prescribed, but the terrors of abuse and being taken over continued. I was seeing her four times a week and speaking with her on the fifth day, trying to create a sufficiently safe haven for her to express, contain, and understand her terrors. While she typically turned to me for safety, support, and understanding, when her paranoid fears became most intense, she became fearful that I, too, would torture her or attempt to control her for my own purposes. During one poignant moment when she was curled up in a ball on the chair and sobbing, feeling utterly helpless and hopeless in dealing with these terrors, I happened to tilt my rocking chair ever so slightly forward. Startled, she placed her hands up on the wall as if trying to climb to safety. I had a sense of a little girl being physically beaten and having nowhere to turn but to the wall. I calmly described the events that had just occurred and how she appeared to feel so unsafe and terrified. When she had gradually calmed, together we spoke about the power of her fears and of their relational origins.

During this particular period, however, her suicidal terror, her impulse to jump to freedom, intensified. Because she was living alone, we agreed, to the relief of both of us, that she needed a hospital to create a sufficiently safe place in which she could experience all of the emergent terrors and not feel all alone, but safe, so as to integrate her previously dissociated affects and memories. As part of this reintegration process, she needed a place, unlike a private office setting, where she could scream out the full intensity of her terror and rage.

Comment: Our dyad was serving as an oasis in a sea of dangerous turbulence, and the respect we each had for the initiative of the other allowed Samantha to participate as a partner in our *cooperation* around the recommendation for hospitalization. In terms of the incident in the office, Samantha, basing herself on her prior lived experience of danger and abuse, *predicted* my rocking chair movement indicated an incipient attack. Based on my lived experience with her increasing trust in me, I *predicted* my gentle description would facilitate her calming – which involved *repair* and *restoration* of the relationship – even after such a powerful *disruption*.

Fortunately, I was able to find a private hospital that at the time had one floor with a psychoanalytically oriented staff. There she stayed for a month where she worked with a psychologist who, serendipitously, reminded her of me. The hospital served to provide her with the safety needed for her to experience the full range

84   Clinical Guidelines

of her terrifying emotions and memories. She screamed her fear and her rage. She would cower in the corner, sob – and talk. At the hospital she had individual and group treatment, phone sessions with me, and the camaraderie and support of other patients who felt much of the same. All of these supports cocreated a sufficiently safe place, a holding environment (Winnicott, 1965; Slochower, 1996), in which to feel, express, and contain her terrors and rage.

During this period Samantha became terrified of her parents and refused to see them. She had remembered and recognized what had occurred in her family. Toward the end of her stay, she was prepared to see her parents, and she invited them to visit. Her mother, however, declined ostensibly due to other commitments and the meeting failed to take place. Samantha was enraged, and this time expressed herself more assertively to her mother.

When Samantha was discharged, she was fragile, but stable. The terrors had diminished and we proceeded with our analytic work. One year down the line, she anxiously, yet with a sense of triumph, discontinued her medication. Over the next several years, the terrors subsided and our work took on a more even tone. In one dream, she was taking a math class. Realizing that she needed help, she went back to the professor, who was kind and not judgmental, which, she said, reminded her of me.

> He speaks to me quietly, calmly, and my panic subsides. I still do not understand how he explains the process of finding the solution, but at least I feel less frustrated and isolated. He does an entire problem for me, from beginning to end on a page; he writes out all the short steps along the way, leaving nothing out. I watch him write – it is very comforting. He tears the page from his pad. When he is done, he hands it to me. Now I feel I have a way to follow, a frame of reference for the next problem I will be given. I leave feeling relieved, less scared, less frustrated.

In Samantha's dream she envisions a protective, idealizing self-object relationship in which the man is calming and knows how to solve the problem, providing a roadmap for the next problem she'll be facing. She easily related these qualities to her experience with the analyst.

> Comment: Working *cooperatively* together with a protective, older male, which made her feel "less isolated," and *sharing moments of enlivening experience* were evident both in the dream and in the analytic process. Her dream rendering of the professor's skill in meeting her precise

needs draws on the child's *awe and admiration* for the caregiver who knows just what she needs to be successful in carrying out an intention. The affectively laden sense of competence and safety emerging from learning new procedures for dealing with life's problems, in turn, gradually *raised the threshold for negative experience* and *lowered the threshold for positive experience.*

Not working steadily and living alone, Samantha began to feel isolated and in need of more connections with people. She had particularly prized the groups in the hospital where she could just be herself – unlike what had been her usual experience in life. I suggested that she join one of my analytic groups and she did. Group therapy became a place where she could practice being herself and speak her mind.

The themes of feeling judged, controlled, and imposed upon as well as distrust of others all entered the scene at one time or another. Moreover, she became acutely aware of how she, now identifying with parental attitudes, could become the judgmental, controlling "Swiss-German good girl" who imposes her agenda on others. On a number of occasions, the therapy group became the threatening problem-ridden family and she wanted out. These issues were reworked time and again. With evolving self-delineation and freedom, she increasingly was able to respond perceptively and empathically to others.

Her relationship with her parents changed dramatically. A joint session with her mother facilitated communication. She spoke far more directly and assertively with her parents. She skillfully extricated herself from her parents' attempts to use her in their power struggles. Once, her mother tried to give her an art object of her father's. Noticing her father wince, Samantha objected that her mother had not asked him and turned to her father and inquired about his feelings. As she was able to hold her own with them and not feel overwhelmed, she was better able to accept their limitations and to receive what they had to offer. In turn, her parents appeared to become more often directly loving and supportive.

Comment: Samantha was able to help her parents reflectively process feelings that, in this instance, averted a possible *disruption* between her parents when her mother took action that was potentially injurious to her father and that might have evoked a rage reaction. From a dynamic systems perspective it would be expected that as one member of a family changes, in this instance Samantha, it might alter the family system and lead to change in the other individual family members. In addition, she was increasing her capacity to *predict* her own reactions as well as those of others.

86 Clinical Guidelines

Samantha began to date again. She seemed to have little difficulty in meeting men and in becoming romantically involved. She became more aware, however, of her tendency to rush into passionate sexual relationships with men before she developed more fundamental emotional connections. Gradually, as she became less expectant of being controlled and terrorized and, in turn, more willing to risk emotionally exposing herself, her relationships with men deepened.

> Comment: Samantha was becoming able to attach in more complex ways: She was less frozen and more affectively present. Using more balanced sensuality and sexuality she was now able to forge a more lasting romantic connection. This contrasted with her previous attempts to enter into attachments more or less exclusively through sexual passion. Her balanced sensual/sexual connecting with men was more in keeping with *social norms* and enabled her to cocreate *shared enlivening experiences*.

After four years of analysis, Samantha had improved considerably. She felt much better about herself and more alive. Her affective experience was more available to her and more manageable. Her trust in me had grown immeasurably, and she was becoming more expressive of affectionate feelings for me. At the end of one session, she inquired at the door if it would be okay to give me a hug. She said that she was feeling close and wanted to thank me for hanging in there with her. Clearly she was initiating the hug; with affection I received her hug and hugged her back – something that is comfortable for me when it feels as fitting as it did at this moment. For both of us, this was a poignant hug that powerfully communicated trust, affection, and gratitude. I was particularly struck by it, for, as we discussed in the following session, it was an expression of her trust that neither of us would misinterpret the hug. It was like a watershed after what she had come through in her previous analysis. Subsequently, Samantha upon parting after sessions either extended her hand for a handshake, or wanted to have a brief hug, or else preferred, especially when she was upset with me, to have no contact at all. Our routine for parting developed in such a way that she could initiate whatever form of physical contact occurred to her as fitting and articulate her feelings as well. I was convinced that this variable routine broadened her affective experience, sense of safety, and the intimate connection between us. We were moving into what has been called intersubjective relatedness (Benjamin, 1988, 1995; Fosshage, 1997a, 2003; Shane, Shane, & Gales, 1998; Stern, 1985), a realm of relating that requires an expanded expression of the analyst's subjective experience to create a more reciprocal (yet, still asymmetrical) subject-to-subject intimacy.

> Comment: Research on the topic of physical *touch* in psychoanalysis (summarized in Fosshage, 2000) indicates that hugs initiated by the patient are experienced as therapeutic while hugs initiated by the analyst tend to engender distrust. The analyst's responsiveness to the patient's initiative to hug can cocreate *an authentic sense of being known* as well as a *shared moment of enlivened lived experience*.

After four years of analysis, Samantha had the following dream, which gave us a sweeping vision of what had been occurring. The dream was presented in three parts as follows:

> I. A village – it extends up (and down) a slope. It is not a steep slope, but gradual and graceful; it is feminine. It is winter. I am looking down on the village as if on a model train set. I see their roofs; they look like old leather books perched on each house. There are train tracks that wind through the village, unifying and connecting it, making it whole.
>
> There are green pine forests, main streets, central squares, country roads hidden under the snowfall. It is quiet, peaceful, lovely. I know that I am the village as well as hovering above it. It is the landscape of myself.
>
> II. A feeling of fear. I am filled with the kind of terror that sent me to the hospital. It is huge, unmanageable, overwhelming. It is all over me; I feel it on my skin, and inside of me. I am paralyzed with fright. This fear is old, familiar. The village goes into a state of suspended animation. It is frozen and still; there is no movement. The me that is in the village ceases to feel. I have the familiar sensation of fear followed by an absence of feeling.
>
> III. Time has passed like in the telling of the Rip Van Winkle story. There is the feeling of 20 years (but I know it has been more) going by. The village has remained in its state of suspended animation. I have lived without feelings all this time.
>
> There is a thaw; the village comes back to life. The cottages are in the same place but feel as if they have been moved to new locations. The relation of the train tracks to the villages and cottages looks the same when I view it from above, but the me that is *in* the landscape feels different. I am disoriented, but not afraid. I am thankful that the frozen sleep is over. There are icicles

melting under the eaves of the cottages; the light falls with a different slant on the landscape.

At the end of the dream I am only in the landscape, no longer above it. I am finding my way through unfamiliar terrain. The thaw has caused patches of earth to appear from under the snow. The landscape is no longer pristine as it was in the beginning of the dream (when it was a model . . . a model child), but I feel grounded in it; it is much more real and filled with vitality.

We understood the dream as depicting a dramatic story of an ongoing psychological transformation. The Rip Van Winkle sleep of 20 years had begun when Samantha was 19, the beginning of adulthood, as she put it, and also the age when she met her former husband, although, as she notes in the dream, she had been asleep longer. Brought up as the model child, she was graceful and feminine, and had achieved some peacefulness but at the cost of being "wintry" and distant from her own experience ("I know that I am the village as well as hovering above it"). In the analysis Samantha began to reconnect with feeling, encountered terror, and, as in the past, froze to put a stop to it. Gradually as we understood and helped her work her way through the fear, she began to thaw, to be "within" her experience, and to become more alive.

Over the past three years, Samantha has pursued her writing and has more and more successfully maintained her focus. Publications have been the reward that have given added reinforcement and incentive. Along the way she shared her writing. I have felt appreciative and affirming of it. As is apparent from her dreams, she is highly capable with images and language. She knew that I wrote and inquired about it. We shared our writings and our experiences about writing. The sharing provided times of mutual recognition, of a twinship experience – moments of intimacy involving intersubjective or subject-to-subject relatedness. Here we were clearly one person to another with mutual respect, affection, and concern for one another.

Comment: Sharing our writings and our experiences about writing provide us with "moments of meeting" (Stern et al., 1998), or what in this book we call *shared enlivening moments*. Included were *moments of mutual surprise and admiration*.

As the age of 40 was closing in, Samantha became quite upset about the prospects of not having children. She was the last hope for her family. While she felt her parents would be disappointed in her not having children, with my encouraging nudge she spoke with them and discovered, to her surprise, that they were not invested in grandchildren, but in *her* happiness. She developed what was for her the best romantic relationship to that point, but the man already had children and did not wish to embark on that path again. Due to a variety of serious setbacks in the man's life, the relationship came to an end.

Subsequently, Samantha and a close male friend began to express their loving and sexual feelings for one another. He was in the process of extricating himself from another relationship. His and Samantha's relationship progressed and began including sexual intimacy. One day Samantha came in excitedly and said, "Jim, I am finally getting sex and a relationship together." Samantha's announcement of this remarkable progress additionally ushered in an increased intimacy in our own relationship. As we explored the new experience she was having with a man we were also able to express positive feelings for each other. She could do this more easily, for she now felt that the playing field between us was level. It was more person-to-person and, yet, asymmetrical (Aron, 1996).

Comment: Over the years of psychoanalytic treatment the tensions between us gradually ameliorated, *ruptures were more quickly repaired*, and reflective awareness was more easily recovered when lost. In addition, *the lowered threshold* for positive experience gave rise to a lightness, to a considerable increase in *humor and play* between us. Our acknowledging the effect of these positive changes on each of us promoted further developments in the areas of *sharing moments of enlivened lived experience, heightened affective moments*, and enhancing *an authentic sense of being known.*

Samantha decided to take a high-paying, full-time position in the arts, heading up her own department. She had become more financially conscious and responsible and wanted to have material things for herself. She had built a good reputation for herself and negotiated admirably. In closing I will present in summary form a recent session with some detailed exchanges that occurred the morning after her first day of work. The context of our having worked for a considerable time together needs to be kept in mind in reading the summary, for analyst and analysand are now dealing rather quickly with primary thematic issues as they emerge in the session, currently triggered by her new job. These issues are quite familiar to us and we have mutually developed a reflective awareness, conceptualization, and vocabulary in regard to them. During the session Samantha was clearly struggling with the now long recognized thematic battle between being herself and being controlled by those around her and by the corporate structure.

90   Clinical Guidelines

Samantha opens the session by saying, "This is the first full-time job since 1991 and I am stressed." I inquire, "What's the stress?" She responds, "Fear of being trapped." I ask, "In what way?" She describes how she needs to eat every two hours (an extensive use of antibiotics had totally dysregulated her system) and does not want to reveal it, for it places her in a weakened position as the head of a department with people she does not know. We discuss how her response to being physically dysregulated on the first day at work is understandably upsetting; Yet, her reaction also appears to resonate with her own perfectionism (and with self-attributions based on being "the perfect child"). After focusing on various practical alternatives, Samantha ends up poignantly saying that she does not want to be at her new job and wants to go home. I continue to explore: "Any other reasons?" She responds, "It's boring, unsafe. I don't know what I'm doing." She relates it to feeling trapped in school, bored and inhibited. With her freelance jobs, she could be in for six months and then "out of there." In a somewhat pleading tone of not wanting to be forced to do it, she reiterates "boredom, claustrophobia, and complexity of relationships." I emotionally join her and reflect, "Yes, in a freelance situation, you can work six months and then get out of there and you're fine." She says, "Yes, and I could continue to do that. Why should I have to face forced commitment? My commitment to you comes out of desire, need; I love you and, if we have difficulties, we work them out." I respond, "That's a new model, a new way of doing things, in contrast to what it often felt like at home." She answers, "At home I felt driven to be something I'm not. I'm not fully myself. I had to perform perfectly at home." I reiterate a vision of being that we both know and she has momentarily lost touch with: "Maybe you don't have to be so perfect at work; maybe you could take some time to absorb, familiarize, get your footing." She picks up the message, "You know I only need a pad and pencil until I figure out what I'm doing." She describes several interactions in which she was honest and "not perfect" and then says, "I feel like killing my father. The perfectionism came from him." And then with a slightly helpless tone, "I'm disappointed that it's so deep." I respond, "Yeah, that's the way it is. That's what happens when these neural networks get activated." (Neural networks are something that we have discussed in detail.) We discuss again how one has to regain a reflective awareness of a theme and its origins to free oneself from its grip – in this case the feeling of perfectionist expectations. She is reminded of how as a girl she would sneak out of her window onto the roof – to be alone, smoke, and regain her equanimity. I respond, attempting to open up a new avenue, "Yes, there you couldn't solve it in the relationship; now, perhaps you can; perhaps you can just *be*, and then you can be at home wherever you go." She responds with feeling, "That would be wonderful." There is a reflective pause. And then she declaims flatly yet with satisfaction: "You know we did it! Thank you, I can breathe again!"

The theme of perfectionism, of being the model child, had once again been activated and, old hands as we were by this time, we were relatively quickly able to help her regain a perspective on it and to reclaim a sense of freedom from the perfect-child self-attribution. In my responses, I reminded her of an alternative vision and way of "being" that had previously been achieved and to which she could now emotionally relate. Confirmation of this momentary success came in the group therapy session, four days later, in which she relayed what had happened and how "happy" she had been since the last session.

Looking back, Samantha and I had traveled a remarkably long way together. Virtually all of the 12 developmental capacities and qualities we have described earlier were involved in the transformative analytic experience. Central was the recognition of the parentally imposed attributions, the way she was "bred," which felt so incongruous to her "inner integral self." Despite the traumatic imposition of her parents' agenda, an imposition that fragmented her self-narrative, Samantha was able to maintain some sense of an authentic self along with a considerable determination to develop, to realize her authentic self one way or another. Processing and repairing traumatic ruptures both within and outside the analytic relationship contributed to a growing sense of competence and self-regulation as well as a sense that others could be helpful rather than just a source of further upset. Our close tracking of her experience, emphasizing affects, meanings, intentions, and goals, contributed to her extricating herself from the parental attributions and to articulating and consolidating a more cohesive narrative of her authentic self, all occurring first and foremost within, but not by any means limited to, the analytic relationship in which she could gradually experience being seen and known by the analyst.

As she consolidated a more cohesive, positive sense of an authentic self or, in other words, as she became more fully her own person, Samantha gradually desired a fuller relationship in the analysis with the entrance of more of my subjectivity, which was now no longer terrifying to her. Our subsequent experiences of sharing moments of enlivening experience and heightened moments of surprise, awe, and admiration were based on, as she expressed it, "a level playing field." With the increased sharing of our subjective experiences with one another, analysis become one person to another (subject-to-subject relating). Now affection could be mutually experienced and expressed both verbally and through physical touch. Hugs and handshakes, initiated by Samantha, were potent affective communications. Each had a distinctive meaning, fit to the occasion, serving to regulate the closeness between us as well as increasing her sense of personal agency, her experience of being a "doer doing." These verbal and physical expressions of affection emanated from a hard-won profound sense of safety and self-assuredness that stood in contrast to the previous traumatic childhood and analytic transgressions. Humor and playfulness contributed their share to an ambiance of lightness in our sessions. Overall her originally high threshold for experiencing positive emotions was lowered and her low threshold for negative affects was raised. The world, self and other, became more enlivened.

50–50?!?

We now offer a second case presentation illustrating a different analytic facilitation of a number of the developmental processes delineated in our first essay.

The mother of a patient of mine (F. L.), Larry, died about a year ago, and sometime later, her will was opened. During the intervening time Larry's older brother said that no matter how their mother allocated the money she left, and it turned out that she left quite a bit, they would split it 50–50. Larry agreed.

Some background. As a child, Larry was bullied, mocked, cheated, and derided continuously by his slightly older brother. This brother also was quite cruel to their mother, whereas Larry was his mother's empathic support. Larry's father had died quite young. Each of the brothers made a career out of his character style. The brother did financially very well on Wall Street while Larry did a lot of good, working with people who needed empathy.

> Comment: Larry's childhood experience reinforced a sense of safety, pride, and competence through his providing reliable caretaking and emotional support within his family, especially for his mother, but, in a way, for his brother as well. The price he paid for his noble qualities was, paradoxically, that they came at the expense of his sense of agency, self-assertion, and initiative.

Earlier, to purchase a new apartment, Larry and his wife had needed a bridge loan until their current apartment sold. Larry asked his brother, who had plenty of available cash, but he refused. When Larry asked him why he refused to give him the loan, the brother said, "Because you didn't ask me the right way." You get the picture of Larry's brother.

Now comes the will. The mother left three times more money to Larry than to his brother. I thought she knew what she was doing. Larry believed that since he had already agreed to the 50–50 split he was now obligated to honor it. I asked him, "Why?" We then spent many months with my arguing, "It's your mother's last will." My objections ran contrary to Larry's whole life of having been the good, honorable guy, the conciliatory caretaker, someone who would never go back on his word. I also insisted that this was a rare opportunity, a once-in-a-lifetime event, that afforded him a choice. He had a chance to act in his legitimate self-interest rather than succumbing to the pressure of others. We had been working on Larry's accommodation to various people in his life, and its cost to him. In that context I had already said to him, "I think you would be much better off suffering from an excess of sadism than an excess of masochism."

Comment: In the therapeutic context of self-regulation and interactive regulation, the impact of humorous, mild-to-severe violations of expectations organize *heightened affective moments*. In my interventions, I tried to perturb the rigid system of compliance and accommodation to the needs of others. Furthermore, Larry understood I was not being literal (though I was serious about the will). *Metaphoric processes* transfer cognitive and emotional meanings through the recognition of implicit and explicit similarities and dissimilarities of lived experience. Our communicating through metaphor and analogy enriched the sense of self and a further expansion into the world of imaginative possibilities. I had in mind Kohut's definition of self as the center for initiative that can lead to a more balanced use of *cooperation*, without self-sacrifice or pathological accommodations. As we have described, for the infant, spontaneous *initiating and cooperating* with initiating others are essential to forming an adaptive agentic sense of self. In a similar vein, for the patient in treatment, initiation and exploration can generalize to other areas of life. In this case the hope was that Larry's experiences with me might contribute to *his* agentic sense of self.

Larry's brother placed enormous pressure on him to give him half the inheritance, even taking him for a session to see his, the brother's, therapist. I said to Larry, relying on my years of experience watching *Law and Order* reruns, that his initial agreement was made under pressure and like a confession made under duress, it would not stand up in court. Larry pleaded: "How could I do this to my brother. He'll never speak to me again." We went over his lifelong experiences with his brother many times, and he had to agree that if, indeed, his

94   Clinical Guidelines

brother had expected to receive the greater inheritance, he, the brother, would never have proposed the 50–50 split. Furthermore, if his brother never spoke to him again, would it be a great loss? And so, eventually, the money and goods left by the mother were distributed according to the specifications of her will. The brother felt betrayed and Larry developed panic attacks, fainting spells, and claustrophobia.

We linked these symptoms to the stand he took vis-à-vis his brother. Pleading with me to let him give his brother half the money, he said, "Look at the symptoms I developed by not giving my brother half the money." I said, "Yes, but can you imagine what symptoms you would have developed if you had given the money to your brother?" Considering that prospect helped somewhat, but the light-headedness and panic attacks continued.

> Comment: Although in the throes of panic-like anxiety Larry could see the humor in my intervention and he enjoyed its audacious quality, which was reinforced through a negotiating process on which we embarked. Larry kept reducing the extra amount he would give his brother – $100,000 to $50,000 to $25,000 – but I was adamant. Not a penny. Later he commented that if he had given him any extra money he would never have become his own person.

We spoke about the symptoms he developed as being similar to those of his mother due to her eventually fatal brain tumor. I said that his symptoms resurrected his mother and restored contact with her. But more to the point, in not yielding to his brother's pressures, Larry had changed his whole world. It was now not the same world in which he grew up. Furthermore, his actions not only destabilized him but made him feel that he was behaving like his brother. All of this exploration helped a bit yet his symptoms persisted. They tended to become particularly strong in confined places such as at a table in a restaurant or sitting in the middle seat of a row at the theater.

His panic in a confined space led us back, again, to a trauma at age 14. Larry had gotten into a car with a group of friends. He realized that the driver of the car, a teenager, was quite drunk. He thought about not getting into the car but could not get himself to say "I won't" to his friends. The car smashed into a tree and Larry, in the backseat, suffered very severe injuries. He was confined to a hospital bed, in traction, a halo drilled into his skull to let the neck injuries heal. He lay confined without being able to move for several weeks.

The panic attacks occurred in places in which he felt confined, unable to get out. It reminded him of feeling trapped, unable to move, in the hospital bed. But now, when he felt the panic come on, he could escape, dash out of the restaurant into the fresh air and that would help. In the theater he tried to sit in an aisle seat so he could get out without disturbing anyone. He said, "If I were to sit in the middle of the row, I would not be able to get up and go out when I need to." I said, "Why not just push your way past the sitting people and get out if you have to." He protested, "I would be disturbing everyone." I said, "You have great difficulty being obnoxious." We both laughed and what I did not say I think was implicit for both of us, "like your brother." He said that he had concert tickets with his wife during the next week and he had gotten aisle seats. I said, "That's cheating. If you do have to get up to leave, you have to go down the row of seats to the other aisle, past all the sitting people."

> Comment: Children learning, understanding, and internalizing the rules of social norms facilitates their ability to *predict* the actions and response of others and themselves across a widening spectrum of contexts, including a therapeutic experience. The pretend rules I made up, to cut across all the seats to the other aisle, challenged Larry to relax the rigid rules that made him adhere to his misguided *social conventions*. Furthermore I presented a scenario to Larry whereby he could overcome his dread of being pushy and annoying, and aggressively promote his bid for self agency.

My scenario prompted Larry to announce, "I am feeling light-headed right now. I may have to leave." I said, "What if I stand in front of the door and block it?" He answered, "I would probably just lie down on your couch and dissolve." I said, "You mean you wouldn't push me out of the way?" After a pause he said, "You're formidable."

> Comment: Wanting to leave could be viewed as a *disruption*. It could be viewed as my having gone too far in my effort to challenge Larry's pathologically accommodating stance. However, rather than joining Larry in a retreat from self-assertion, I upped the ante. Having previously questioned why Larry had to "protect" the other people sitting in his row if he were to push himself past them to get to the aisle, I thought that I should not be exempt from being pushed or inconvenienced. Larry would have to imagine pushing me, touching me, aggressively, in his bid for self-agency. Humor provides a way of exploring the world through imagination and *metaphor*. For the infant, exploration of the world through sight, sound, taste, feel, or smell, or by grabbing or holding leads to an experience of agency. For Larry, having parents who failed to protect him

96 Clinical Guidelines

from his bullying brother, and having a mother who needed him to comfort and protect her from the brother's abuse, curtailed his freedom to explore. Depicting Larry's world through the lens of humor challenged his self-sacrificing caretaking and opened up exploratory possibilities. Referring to me as "formidable" provided him with the temporary protection whereby his sense of safety, efficacy, and competence could evolve in its unique design. Furthermore, such *heightened affective moments* of lived experience whether they emerge from an action by a caregiver and infant, or analyst and patient, elicit a positive surprise, a feeling of *awe*, and *appreciation and admiration* of the caregiver and analyst.

The panic attack was over – never to return again. In fact, neither has the light-headedness nor have the fainting episodes, although Larry worries still about their possible recurrence. We have continued to focus on his pushing people out of the way so as not to feel trapped and, in general, becoming more comfortable with being obnoxious, and not so accommodating.

Comment: Some of my interventions may sound similar to what is referred to as "flooding" in Behavior Modification treatments where the patient is encouraged to actually engage, repetitively, in the situation that evokes anxiety. The aim is desensitization. In my interventions I did not actually mean for Larry to go across the row of seats to another aisle. We were playing seriously, or seriously playing. In the "as if" situation of our play he was able to experience the anxiety as though he were in the actual situation. We relocated his "real world" in his internal subjective world, and he felt the anxiety even though we were both just sitting in my office. Herein lies the therapeutic action of humor. Shared humor makes absurd circumstances feel real and evokes the feelings that actual circumstances evoke.

Larry and I shared his lived experience, standing up to his brother and holding his own. He felt I was with him and that I shared his experience, which produced a sense of commonality and safety.

Reflections

It may seem surprising that in treatment one can chart the continuing trajectories of capacities and qualities that have their beginning in the first year of life. And yet this is what we see once we shift the center of inquiry to the self as a doer doing, explicated in terms of motivational systems. It is not merely that the motivational systems go back to infancy, but that the experiences of the agentic self also begin there. These experiences, for better or worse, shape the kinds of responses a person becomes capable of as life goes forward, while new experiences along the way make their own contributions, again for better or worse, to the agentic sense of self that the patient ultimately brings to treatment. A person's sense of self, as a doer doing, does not develop in a linear way, but it does develop and it does have its foundation in the first year in ways that are detectable in treatment.

With the focus shifted to the self, especially where the self is defined in terms of an agentic self, a doer doing, our understanding of treatment also shifts. What comes into view are the motivational systems as that which animates the self with feelings, intentions, and goals. And what matters therapeutically is whether the patient can find empathic resonance for his or her experiences as a doer doing. This is the avenue for enlivening the self. But, it also, as this discussion has tried to illumine, allows the therapist and the patient to take a living inventory of qualities and capacities that originated in the first year of life and continue, in whatever form, down to the present. It is not a question of reconnaissance here, nor of genetic reconstruction, but of appreciating the patient as an agent in the present. To this end it helps if the analyst can proceed with an understanding of how the self grows, and has grown, and needs and wishes to grow in the future – and how that process can be charted in action during the treatment. There are, of course, many ways, and many levels, in which and through which one can address the agentic self and foster its enlivening. These ways include the exploration of current and developmental traumas that allow for a raising of the threshold for negative affect. We saw this happen with Samantha. With Larry, we observed rather a kind of metaphoric and playful exploration of seemingly dreaded possibilities that allowed him to become more assertive. But an understanding of the 12 capacities and qualities from early life that we have identified makes for a unifying backdrop to the varieties of therapeutic intervention in terms of their common impact on enlivening the agentic self. To repeat what we said at the outset of this essay, therapeutic change is inextricably entwined with development. To enhance developmental processes is central to therapeutic change. To understand what is being changed requires appreciation of prior development and what has subsequently occurred.

Chapter III

The Wandering Mind

The three of us – Joe Lichtenberg, Frank Lachmann, and Jim Fosshage – have now coauthored four books in which we have stretched Kohut's conceptualization of a psychology of the self in various directions. Central to our work has been the expansion of a theory of motivation. In this book, we have continued this expansion with special emphasis on what goes right in development, but not to the exclusion of how things can go awry. In this endeavor we again recruited a number of familiar concepts, including motives, intentions, actions, experiences, and goals, with an emphasis on their contributions to the optimal functioning, the feeling of aliveness, of the person.

Our starting point right along has been phenomenology. But it is a phenomenology that has been enriched by clinical observation, infant research, and neuroscience. Within that framework, we have continued to focus on the phenomenology of lived experience. That encompasses not only conscious awareness, but nonconscious and unconscious modes of experiencing, with each mode influencing the others. Through our focus on lived experience we have gained a vantage point for considering the neonate, infant, child, adolescent, and adult as a *doer doing*, initiating, and responding in a relational world. We have attempted to describe the worlds in which each doer lives, and the relationship of the doer doing to the origins of the sense of self. In each stage, and in each "world" of experience, our understanding of "doing" has consistently referred to involvement in tasks that involve affect, intentions, and goals.

In this essay, we will extend that perspective by adding to our prior accounts of unfolding motivation (Lichtenberg et al., 2011) an understanding of the significance of the *nontask* focused or *wandering mind* – the misnamed "mind at rest." In that context we will describe varieties of mind wandering. Since our core concepts center on the wide-ranging use of *agency*, our depiction of *a doer doing* includes the process of a person responding mentally and physically to stimulation from one's body and from one's relationship to the other as well as from the patterns of behavior the person himself initiates. As will be clear shortly, our understanding of mind wandering in terms of the self also involves this sort of "feedback," only considered at a different level.

In the discussion that follows, we focus on several important areas of study that are germane to "mind wandering," which we consider represents an important function of the mind as a doer. (In our Afterword we will present a diagrammatic portrayal connecting motivational systems with mind wandering.) This book constitutes our "first word" on the subject of mind wandering. As we began to learn about "mind wandering" research and the varieties and implications of mind wandering, especially its place in adaptive enlivened lived experience, we were blown away. We want to introduce our readers to this fascinating and potentially mind-expanding area of study. We do not intend this to be a "last word" on this subject, to be all-inclusive. Rather, we want to be evocative and hope we can excite, or at least enliven, our reader to study these topics further and to experiment with their clinical applicability.

The Mind at a Task

Up till now, the mind at a task has been central in our discussions such as in our most recent book, *Psychoanalysis and Motivational Systems: A New Look* (Lichtenberg et al., 2011). We have proposed seven motivational systems (exploratory and assertive, sensual and sexual, attachment, caregiving, affiliative, physiological regulation, and aversive through withdrawal and antagonism) that organize and are organized by the sense of self. These motivational systems are engaged in the tasks that the doer does. The doing mind focuses. It may anticipate correctly or incorrectly, learn, and perfect a skill. This process of performing a task sharpens, articulates, strengthens, and in various ways promotes both cohesiveness and flexibility of the sense of self. There is a reciprocal relationship between "doing" and the experience of a sense of self.

Here is an illustration of the analyst as a doer, in this instance engaging empathically with a patient. The empathy illustrates the analyst's mind engaged in a task. An analyst who takes on the task of empathic listening simultaneously also engages a number of other motivational systems implicitly in the listening process. That is, the analyst will, consciously or implicitly, maintain openness to his own exploratory motivations, keeping alive a spirit of inquiry, as well as engage his attachment motivational system. Furthermore, empathy, in addition to requiring a capacity to listen, requires letting in the experience and state of the other. Here our capacity for sensual and sexual pleasure as well as aversive motivations may figure in as we

The Wandering Mind 101

sense ourselves into the narrative we hear. Up to this point we are following Kohut (1981) in not assigning a value to empathy. But as therapists, analytic empathic listening also draws on our capacity to engage in a caring interaction.

An example of a session follows in which a patient, Edgar (treated by J.L.), described how he challenged his wife for the first time about her abusive language to him and their son. Drawing on his understanding of the basis of his timidity and passivity that had been worked on in prior sessions, Edgar commented that he could act now. He was no longer terrified that his wife, like his mother, would collapse into a depression and that his father would blame him for it. Edgar described how difficult it was for him to maintain his determination and not be put off by his wife's protests, threats, and denials. He reported that by evening the atmosphere had cleared and they had one of the best nights together in years, just like when they first met.

I (J.L.) placed myself within Edgar's point of view and could listen quite easily to the unfolding of the event. I could readily apprehend the intersubjective interplay and sense Edgar's pride in having me witness his accomplishment. Without losing the thread of listening to him, I could momentarily shift to an appreciation of his pride in the impact of our prior analytic exploration. I could respond to Edgar's desire for mirroring of his accomplishments. We could share a sense of commonality, of working together. I could accept and experience pleasure in the implied idealization of me for having been helpful.

The session illustrates a traditional and familiar professional route toward developing the analyst's cohesive, temporally continuous, and affectively positive sense of self. Even when an analyst's attention is loosely and flexibly floating, he or she maintains a tie to the connection with the analysand and to the task. In this context, being distracted, wandering too far from connection and task, being "off in space," would be detrimental to the analysis, to the task of empathic listening, and antithetical to the organization of the analyst's sense of self. The quality of focused attention that is required so that performing a task can lead to increased competence and self-satisfaction would be absent. In contrast to the ease of the task of listening to these "leading edge" associations (Lachmann, 2008; Miller, 1985; Tolpin, 2002) as Edgar recounted his success, at particularly challenging moments in a treatment, a looser, more reverie-like focus may open the analyst to more spontaneous and creative interventions

With respect to empathic listening, our point is this: At rare cool moments of mutual understanding, analysts can place themselves in the state of mind of the analysand with relative conviction and a comfortable sense of connection. At these moments, a sensual tone may prevail like the chord struck by an attuned caregiver and child, as the analyst is listening with undivided focused attention and simultaneously resonating affectively with the patient's experience. This is a familiar and relatively easy application of empathic listening.

The mind at a task is familiar in ordinary life. A person going into an office for a job interview may think about his or her appearance, clothing and stance, what facial expression to reveal (not too eager but not uninterested). Motivations related to physiological regulation, needs for affiliation, exploration, and assertion may all be recruited with varying degrees of intensity. Aversive motivations, such as resentment about having to seek employment, will need to be kept in check. Or, a father and young son constructing a Lego toy together will focus on following the instructions, looking for the appropriate pieces, fitting them together, and checking the correctness of their efforts against the depicted model. Pattern matching and motivations of physiological regulation, dexterity in particular, and attachment and exploration will all be recruited. Assertiveness on the part of the father may have to be kept in check, since the task is a joint one and the attachment of the father to the son will, hopefully, dictate that the father not take over the task.

The Wandering Mind

We now turn to the opposite of focused attention, to the wandering mind. One of the most famous, and exquisitely sensitive, demonstrations of mind wandering in literature is the musings of Stephen Dedalus, the hero of James Joyce's *Ulysses*. Daniel Goleman (2013) considers Joyce's *Ulysses* to be an exquisitely sensitive depiction of a musing mind, a mind that is at play, focused, and yet unfocused as Dedalus monitors his thoughts without reining them in. Surprisingly, however, precisely this is an aspect of "mind wandering" that has recently been studied scientifically.

Our minds obviously can and do wander when we are not focused on a task. Then, we daydream, "woolgather," or, as did Stephen Dedalus, muse. When we come out of such a state we may or may not be aware of where we were in our thoughts or what feeling, memory, or issue we had been wondering about. Our minds may wander in relatively bounded time frames. For example, while waiting for a train we may think about where we are going, where we have been, or where we would prefer to go. While sitting on a beach we might think: Who is that over there? Do I know her (or him)? Where have we met? It's getting hot – shall I go for a dip? I'm so comfortable I hate to move; maybe I'll eat something; I'm feeling a bit bored; I'll take out my book. I really should do that bit of work I brought along. These illustrations center on past, present, and future, and have the person, the doer, the "I," at their center. If you think we made up these illustrations to make our point, try musing on your own and see if you don't also find that you are wandering predominantly around yourself in ruminations about your past, present, and future experiences. For example, see if in the morning between doing tasks your mind wanders with shadows of how your night was and what you're going to do during the day. See if later in the day you have a brief moment of mind wandering about your sense of feeling good or not so good about events of the moment. See if in the evening another bit of mind wandering tells you about your happiness or disappointment in your love life. In the aggregate the three, four, five, or six episodes of mind wandering captured in this way will let you take stock of your sense of self in the context of the moment extending backward and forward in time. You are self-regulating across a spectrum of fluctuating affects, intentions, and goals while regulating your interactions in virtual reality, observing yourself in relatedness through the eyes, or rather "I"s, of your desires, hopes, and plans. In line with our overall approach, in studying mind wandering, we are addressing the phenomenology of the doer doing.

Mind wandering relates directly to the sense of self. Through letting our minds wander, disconnected from a task, we, as doers, are still doing. We are checking in with the status of our sense of self in its multitude of relations and connections. That is, we hold that mind wandering, within boundaries, may actually play a crucial role in adaptation through maintaining and enlivening the sense of self. Research findings from neurophysiology are bringing us this news.

But first, here are definitions of some new and some familiar terms.

Mind wandering is defined as engaging in mental events that are unrelated to current demands, no matter whether from sources within us or from the external environment. Mind wandering involves two core processes. One process is *perceptual decoupling*, the capacity to disengage one's attention from a perceptual task. The other process is *metacognition*, the ability to take explicit note of the current or recent content of one's consciousness – that is, to know whither we wandered.

Here is another illustration: As we read a book or article or even as you read this discussion, your mind may suddenly shift to contemplating a visit to a friend; you might then shift to a time in the past when you visited that friend and a difficult moment that arose during that time. And then you may shift back again to what you are reading. Neuroscientific researchers consider these shifts in imaginative thought as unrelated to external circumstances. Here we are *decoupling* our thoughts from our external circumstances. However, as psychoanalysts we might

104 The Wandering Mind

be able to infer an underlying connection among these "associations" or flights of fancy. As psychoanalysts we would, of course, be interested in the meanings of the thoughts and places to which we wander. For the present discussion, however, we will not pursue the preconscious and unconscious connections among the associations but instead consider the process of mind wandering itself, as do the neuroscientists. Upon reflection we may even be surprised when we note – and that "noting" is a reflection, a metacognition – just how far our mind has wandered. Mind wandering thus involves two kinds of fluctuations in attention. The processes at work here, decoupling of our mind and subsequent metacognition and perception, depend on a pair of reciprocal mental shifts so that information that is apparently unrelated to our current situation can gain prominence in our conscious thoughts. Through metacognition we become aware of fluctuations in the content of consciousness. At least intermittently, we become aware that, and to where, our mind has wandered. Our capacity for metacognition has made the study of mind wandering possible, since people can observe that their mind is wandering and report the content of these mental forays. The content that the wandering mind reveals is technically referred to as "stimulus independent thought."

An international team of researchers (Schooler et al., 2011) has been investigating the phenomena of mind wandering and has proposed two key functions to describe this activity. These two key functions are essential to our ongoing stability and well-being, which is the way the researchers speak about the sense of self. And the two key functions are the aforementioned perceptual decoupling and metacognition or meta-awareness.

To summarize briefly, we have the capacity to disengage perception from attention. This is known as perceptual decoupling. By decoupling perception and attention we can also become aware of what we are currently conscious. This mental capacity is referred to as meta-awareness. One more definition. Mental events, such as thoughts, memories, fantasies, expectations, and anticipations can arise without any external source evoking them. These mental events are known as "stimulus independent thoughts." (A caveat: In our view, the researchers may overstate the totality of decoupling from all external sources. We may never be free of influence from the context in which we find ourselves. So we would rather say mind wandering occurs with minimal influence by context – that is, by external sources.)

Our capacity to disengage attention from whatever we perceive at that moment occurs without conscious intent. The researchers propose that perceptual decoupling "demonstrates that mental events that arise without any external precedent, the stimulus independent thoughts, often interfere with the processing of sensory information" (Schooler et al., 2011, p. 319). Furthermore, that we are aware that our mind has "wandered" indicates that we are only intermittently aware of engaging in mind wandering as it happens. The value in possessing "variations in the coupling between the mind and perception" (Schooler et al., 2011, p. 319) is in allowing information unrelated to the current situation to form the centerpiece of conscious thought. Fluctuations in awareness of the contents of consciousness and in particular a realization that the mind has in fact wandered depend on the intermittent meta-awareness. What these researchers propose is actually quite shocking to us, as analysts. According to the researchers, our minds have a mind of their own.

As the researchers (Schooler et al., 2011) have recently documented, the mind is never at rest, even when we are resting or sleeping. As summarized by Healy (2010) the wandering mind is considered a "default mode network." Marcus Raichle and Abraham Snyder (2007) stated that the sense of self achieves some realization in the brain and in the wandering mind; the default mode network seems to be a critical element of that organization. It captures many of the features of how we think of ourselves as a self. Clearly, when the mind wanders, it does not disconnect totally from one's life and environment; rather it scans, circles through, hops, skips, and jumps to memories and wishes, past, present, and future, but does not disconnect. Optimally, mind wandering is a vitally useful and necessary form of what we might call adaptive (nonpathological) "dissociation." Essentially, mind wandering assures a sense of continuity of an enlivened sense of self over time

Crucial in investigating mind wandering has been the research and identification of stimulus independent thought. Specifically this research has investigated the neural processes that occur in the absence of an explicit task. These are the processes that occur when the mind is just wandering and is in a "resting" state. During this resting state, surprisingly, a neural network comes alive. The neural network that is active at this time is referred to as the default mode network.

To back up a bit. Numerous neural networks respond to different mental activities. Some brain networks are active when we recall past events; other networks are active when we imagine ourselves into the future; and still others are active when we infer the motivations and feelings of other people. But when we daydream all of these networks have been found to resonate together. This conglomerate of neural networks, the default mode network, is believed to function as our brain's neutral setting. And shifting between attention to a task at hand and unrelated or peripheral thoughts or stimuli is the essence of our consciousness.

The neuroscientists (Schooler et al., 2011; Raichle & Snyder, 2007; Smallwood & Schooler, 2006) have come to believe that the default mode network is crucial to maintaining a cohesive, continuous sense of self. In fact they propose that "in the idling brain our concept of self is created, altered, and renewed" (cited in Healy, 2010). Furthermore, they have observed that when we are in this mind-wandering mode, our minds rarely wander very far away from ourselves (from the "I" wonder, "I" hope, "I" remember, "I" intend). The content of the wandering mind is thus integral to the beneficial functions of the wandering activity. Significantly, the neural activity of the mind-wandering state stands in sharp contrast to the neural activity recorded when our brain is at work on a task. When the task-oriented mind is in the ascendance, this mind-wandering activity is suppressed. As we immerse ourselves in a task, the default mode network gets quiet and other networks come on.

Research on the default network and mind wandering has focused the attention of neuroscientists on such "mushy" topics, given their previous perspective, as the sense of self. They are now proposing that the rich inner world can be studied, that our very existence as separate embodied individuals can be observed and investigated. Although early in his work Freud (1996) abandoned his project of linking physical, neurological structures in the brain with psychoanalytic concepts, this very possibility may now be finding support in neuropsychological research (Raichle & Snyder, 2007).

Geneticists (see Lehrer, 2007) once dismissed genes that were found to have no known function as "junk genes" (Lachmann, 2011). It was because the geneticists did not yet know what the "junk genes" did. Similarly, in the past neuroscientists dismissed the "idle" or "idling" brain. Like a car parked with the motor running, the idle brain was not going anywhere, or so the scientists said.

Not so. Raichle et al. (2001) have ascertained in neuroimaging studies that during tasks that required subjects to focus their attention, neural regions that were associated with those tasks became active. But as these subjects relaxed between tasks while still hooked up to the neural image scanners, a large and different group of neurons consistently lit up. The Raichle team noted that part of the neural network that lit up was the network that activates when a person recalled his past (I remember). And another set of neurons also lit up that activate when we try to imagine what another person is thinking (I think he thinks). The scientists proposed that each region of this default network is focused on the self sensed as I, and that the network's activation of personal history and relationships importantly accrues to our self-definition. Furthermore, Raichle et al. proposed that during these periods of zoning out, what we do is to organize principles of interactions with others (how I will deal with her) and navigating in the world (where, when, and how I will do it). We make sense of and react to the information we apprehend such as, for example, someone's intentions toward us, or whether our child is about to make a dangerous move. We make rapid calculations and choices without having to go through a complex series of beliefs, values, and excruciatingly complex observations and assumptions that we have about the people and ourselves in our world. Raichle and colleagues reported another important observation about the default network. It has two sources of blood supply, unlike other neural networks. Having two sources of blood supply makes it less vulnerable to damage from stroke. This attests to its importance. Raichle et al. speculate that zoning out and daydreaming, indulged in at appropriate times, play an important role in our mental well-being. But it also appears to have a bottom-line usefulness, and the value of a balance between a task orientation and a wandering mind has gained recognition even in corporate American. As columnist David Brooks (2013) commented in a *New York Times* op-ed article, nowadays companies hiring employees want to see candidates "who possess the magical combination: a strict work ethic but a loose capacity for 'mind wandering'" (p. A27).

The Mind of a Task-a-holic

In discussing the beneficial aspects of moderate mind wandering, and of a balance between mind wandering and task orientation, we must also consider what happens at the extremes. At one extreme is excessive mind wandering associated with an inability to remain focused on a task, such as in Attention Deficit Disorder (ADD) and Attention Deficit Hyperactivity Disorder (ADHD). Here we might tentatively postulate disorders in mind wandering that limit a person's ability to focus on adaptive intentions and goals. At the other extreme, mind wandering can be drastically curtailed and the person's entire being might be totally focused on task after task. That is, an exclusive focus on tasks at hand precludes the ability to let one's mind wander. Pathologies at this extreme include work-a-holics and other addictive patterns. The case of Roger (treated by J. L.) is illustrative.

Roger, a young bisexual man, sought therapy because of his sexual addiction. When humiliated by his wife and her rich parents for failing to live up to their expectations, he would compulsively cruise for a male prostitute. The addictive pattern entailed having the prostitute perform fellatio. To Roger this meant he was being offered obeisance. We understood this pattern to be Roger's attempt to reverse his prior experience. Rather than being humiliated, he was being idealized through the act and thereby felt able to restore some of his lost self-respect.

Shame was painfully recursive in Roger's life. His repetitive attempt to seek "pride" through the obeisance of another male succeeded for brief moments only to be increased afterward by the very way in which he had tried to dispel the shame. Pressured by his wife and ashamed of his addiction to fellatio, he sought treatment.

Roger was also addicted to work. He attempted to meet his wife's family's expectations and establish a sense of competence for himself by working long hours in his office. He had gradually abandoned his other interests, stopped paying attention to his home life, and ceased responding to the calls and e-mails of friends. Moreover, with the single-minded determination of an addict for his "hit," Roger's total focus at work came to center on what he imagined to be a dazzlingly perfect solution to whatever problem lay at hand. Originally, this kind of "hit" was sought so that others would confirm his brilliance. The sought-after admiration was yet another means for masking his multidetermined shame. Gradually, however, he had become so disconnected from the actual work requirements at his job that the confirmation only existed as a fantasized expectation. To hone his work to perfection he delayed delivery of his work assignments to the point of outraging all his disappointed clients and associates. He imagined that the brilliant product he would deliver would make up for the delay and avert criticisms. In actuality, he couldn't deliver the assignment until he believed it to be perfect, until he covered all eventualities and produced a unique solution. Since none of his associates were perfect enough for him, he could not delegate work. Roger and I recognized that he was in a vicious circle. The more he focused on perfecting his solution to the task, the longer the delay in completing the project, and the less likely his work would be given the recognition he desired. Each time he failed to turn work in added to his shame. To escape the shame he resorted to a yet more intense focus on the task and a still longer delay before completion.

Roger's life, his addictions, and his ways of attempting to mask them were designed to shield him from shame: shame and humiliation from his wife, shame from seeking male prostitutes, and shame through his pursuit of perfection in his work and its disastrous consequences. To engage in mind wandering, even to a modest degree, carried with it the danger of encountering only negative images of himself and profound shame. Roger's focusing feverishly on tasks at hand offered him some protection from having to face the subjective experience of having a terribly low estimate of his self-worth with attendant shame.

Rather than pursue Roger's treatment, per se, we wish to emphasize that for Roger, focusing on a task, exclusively, deprived his sense of self of the essential "nutriments" that mind wandering can provide, including some reflection on positive experiences when they occurred. Having legislated extraneous thoughts and attention out of his mental repertoire, he had no access to self-provided sources of self-esteem enhancement. The more he masked his shame and its sources, the more he focused on the tasks, and the more he sought to find acclaim from others, the more he disappointed them in the length of time he took before delivering his work in a repetitive, never-ending cycle. Roger's sense of self was so suffused in shame that he devoted his waking life to avoiding the self-awareness that individuals ordinarily derive from mind wandering.

Free Association

But, haven't analysts always made use of the value of mind wandering through free association? Our answer is yes and no. Looked at in one way, free association is the opposite of mind wandering. Rather than occurring ad libitum, at one's pleasure, patients are asked, even instructed, to "free" associate. It becomes a purposeful task assigned to a doer. Its purpose is to reveal feelings, intentions, and goals, repressed conflicts, attitudes, and attributions both to oneself and to the other, the analyst. It is directed activity in other words; the goal is to reveal motives. And free association is not directed to reveal just any set of motives, but those, in particular, that the patient does not want to become aware of and those that the patient does not want the analyst to know. Furthermore, the purpose is not only to reveal shameful or guilt-filled motivations, but also to discover the means of not knowing. Looked at this way, free association is clearly task-centered. From this perspective, free association does not involve "decoupling" but rather a new kind of "coupling" by building on a chain of associations. But we can also look at free association another way.

Free association bears a strong resemblance to mind wandering. To pursue this point, we return to our basic premise. Mind wandering allows the person, the doer, to sense his or her state of mind as a doer doing. It takes advantage of metacognition in a way that allows the analysand to report what he or she has been thinking about and feeling about, at that very moment in time. In effect, this is very close to free association in analysis. *If dreams and their seeming purposeless spontaneity are the royal road to the unconscious, then mind wandering is the royal road to articulating and enriching the sense of self.* Free association exploits dreams as a way of staying as close as possible to the spontaneously emerging thoughts and feelings as they "come to mind." In this process, free association parallels the natural enlivening emergent from the wandering of the mind. And, furthermore, like reporting one's dreams, reporting one's free associations may have a salutary effect. Perhaps psychoanalysis has intuitively recognized and exploited the manner in which naturally occurring aspects of

110 The Wandering Mind

dreams and mind wandering can reveal much of what is implicit in lived experience. And, more to the point, these activities can have a beneficial effect in and of themselves.

Meditation

In some of its forms, meditation resembles mind wandering. Like free association, meditation is tasked in that it is done intentionally. On the surface this is contrary to letting the mind wander. In the Buddhist tradition, the goal of meditation is to achieve an altered state of mind, one in which preoccupation with oneself, the I want, and the exigencies of one's daily life, the I am preoccupied with, are transcended and one achieves a spiritual experience. In effect this is just the opposite of letting one's mind wander. However, when meditation is practiced as a complement to psychotherapeutic treatment, the goal is to shift from focusing on the exigencies and problems of work and daily life. In "loosening up" purposefully one gets closer to one's emotional life and one's sense of self. In effect this is similar to mind wandering in that the doer stops doing in the at-a-task sense and gets closer to an apparent random-like preoccupation that relates more intimately with one's inner-self state. The task set is to approach an awareness of oneself, in the here and now, the there and then, and the whenever, as it is lived implicitly as well as explicitly, moment-to-moment, in one's daily life.

In a study by Condon, Desbordes, Miller, and DeSteno (2013) the relationship between altruism and meditation was investigated. After a period of meditation, a group of 20 experimental subjects was led into a room in which they were presumably to wait for a test. In the room were three chairs, two occupied by persons reading newspapers. The subject sat in the empty chair. A woman, a collaborator of the experimenters, entered the room, awkwardly, on crutches, and leaned against the wall. Of the experimental subjects who had previously been given a period of meditation before entering the room 10 offered help, 10 did not. Of 19 subjects in a control group that had no prior period of meditation, 3 offered the disabled woman their chair and 16 did not. The researchers posited that the "noncompassionate" subjects were pulled into inactivity by the influence of the bystander group, the two seated people who ignored the woman and that the "bystander effect" tilted the balance away from empathy for the woman's state.

From the vantage point of our understanding of mind wandering, its connection with meditation, and its positive effect on the sense of self, we propose that the increase in altruism of the subjects who had been exposed to the prior meditation resulted from the opportunity they had to let their minds wander away from daily tasks. We postulate that this drift toward increased awareness of their own emotional state tilted their lived experience toward empathy and sympathy for the crippled woman.

Reading Good Fiction

We now turn to another body of research that is relevant to the relationship between empathy and mind wandering. It is the investigation of the relationship between reading good literature and empathy. This research is part of a broader research paradigm, referred to as *theory-of-mind* studies. These studies investigate our ability to assume a perspective outside our personal frame of reference, to understand others and their frames of reference. Our capacity for empathy is an indication of such a perspective. This area of research can therefore be germane to our investigation of the beneficial effects of mind wandering.

Theory of mind refers to a complex social skill that develops by about age 5 or 6 (Fonagy, 1991; Mayes & Cohen, 1996). Typical studies addressing this theory investigate the age at which children discover that what is in their mind is not necessarily known by others. Usually between ages 5 and 6 children learn they, as do others, have a mind of their own. What they know, what is in their mind, is not necessarily known by others, neither their playmates nor parents. They develop an awareness that they may know something that is not known by others; for example, they might know who took those cookies out of the cookie jar while mom does not. By about age 6 children have come to know how to keep a secret and to lie. Both of these activities affirm that other people's minds have a different content from one's own. An aspect of having a theory of mind is the understanding that one needs to make inferences about what another person may be thinking or what their intentions are. Reading another person's mind one gets a sense of their mental state. This ability is crucial in the development of empathy. And it lately has become clear that reading fiction can have an impact on increasing one's empathic ability, to form more or less accurate inferences about another person's affects, intentions, and goals.

In general, the studies investigating the relationship between reading fiction literature and empathy have compared three groups of subjects. One group is given literary fiction to read, for example, "Chameleon" by Anton Chekhov, *The Round House* by Louise Erdrich, or "Corrie" by Alice Munro. A second group is given popular fiction to read, for example, *Gone Girl* by Gilliam Flynn, *Sins of the Mother* by Danielle Steel, or "Space Jockey" by Robert Heinlein. A third group is given nonfiction to read – for example, "How the Potato Changed the World" by Charles C. Mann, "Bamboo Steps Up" by Cathie Gandel, or "The Story of the Most Common Bird in the World" by Rob Dunn. In some studies a fourth group was included. They read nothing during the time intervals prior to being tested for empathy. Empathy was measured through computerized tests that the subjects took to assess their ability to decode emotions or predict a person's intentions, expectations, or beliefs in a particular scenario.

The subjects who read award-winning and classical fiction scored significantly higher than those who were given popular fiction and nonfiction articles to read. In the study by Castano and Kidd (cited in Belluck, 2013) the subjects who were given literary fiction did better than those who read popular fiction, even though some of the subjects who were assigned to the literary fiction group said they did not enjoy literary fiction. Literary fiction readers also scored better than nonfiction readers. Interestingly, popular fiction readers did as well, or as badly, as the group of subjects who were given nothing to read.

As for explaining the results, Castano and Kidd argue that in popular fiction the author is more in control and focused on plot. In good literary fiction – as, for example, in the works of Chekhov – there is no single authorial voice. Each character represents a different version of reality. The upshot is that the reader has to become more involved, to participate more, which is similar to real life. Literary fiction evokes more imagery on the part of readers and thereby prompted the research subjects to make more use of their own imagery and imagination. This, in turn, prompted them to develop empathy for the literary characters and subsequently their empathic ability became more available. Generally, good literary fiction leaves more to the reader's imagination, prompting the reader to make inferences about the inner life, intentions, and goals of the characters in the story and to be sensitive to emotional nuances and complexity.

The researchers (see Belluck, 2013) also explain that good fiction is character-driven whereas popular fiction is plot-driven. Entering the characters' emotional world in character-driven fiction enlarges the emotional repertoire of the reader. This has ramifications for the reader's self-experience and can in turn enhance self-exploration and curiosity, as well as an understanding of, and empathy toward, others.

From our perspective good fiction would be akin to "guided" mind wandering. The fiction provides a springboard for the reader's mind wandering, but it also veers it, loosely, in both specific and indeterminate directions. In becoming more aware of the inner lives of the literary character, the reader is drawn out of the task-oriented world and into the realms of personal subjectivity; the reader also becomes more aware of the subjectivity of others. These qualities are central to empathy, to developing an awareness of another person's subjectivity, intentions, desires, and feelings as they relate to oneself or others. It is again our contention, as it was with meditation, that there is an intervening variable between reading good literature and empathy: mind wandering. It is mind wandering that increases concern with one's inner life and that of others.

Mind Wandering and the Imaginative Analyst

We have been considering mind wandering in a variety of circumstances and in regard to empathy. We have considered empathic listening as an analytic task, which does not involve mind wandering per se, but we have also illustrated empathy for another in an experimental simulated life situation and suggested that a form of mind wandering might be involved in this case. We turn now to a different sort of example and consider the mind of the doer turning inward, toward spontaneous, imaginative doing, this while functioning empathically as an analyst. To illustrate, let us consider a challenging, affectively intense situation in which the analyst felt threatened for the patient and thus also for himself and the treatment.

As a child, Meg (treated by J. L.) had been subjected to both emotional and physical abuse, mainly by her father. She had struggled through life professionally as well as in her social and romantic relationships. Recurrent disappointments topped whatever successes she achieved. She thereupon resorted to many self-destructive patterns to try to cope with her dysregulated, chaotic affect states. Suicidal inclinations were never far from the surface. Although psychotherapy and medication had helped to reduce many of the self-destructive patterns, she continued to resort to self-cutting when disturbed. Generally Meg cut her wrists; when more upset, she cut her arms and when still more upset, her neck as well.

In the session under discussion, Meg was relating another discouraging episode of having a goal slip away. Nothing I (J. L.) said relieved our shared mounting tension and gloomy foreboding. As the session neared its end the two of us sat in a silence that reflected our mutual momentary helplessness and hopelessness. Through empathic entry into Meg's state of mind I sensed and inferred her depressive preoccupations. Turning to my own mind state, I felt our shared gloom and a shame-laden sense of ineffectualness and desperation. Unexpectedly, I heard myself say: "You are going to cut yourself?!" Meg nodded, "Yes." I said: "Well do it now." Meg looked surprised. I continued: "Do it now! You have a razor blade in your hand. Just do it now." Meg took the imaginary blade and began very delicately to stroke it across her wrist. Then, more firmly and finally with a resolute gesture, she "cut" deeper. As Meg looked intently at her wrist and turned her arm, it was as if both she and I were witnessing drops of blood coming out. Then Meg looked up, sighed deeply, and said, "I'll be all right now" and left. In previous publications we (Lichtenberg et al., 1996) have referred to such interventions as a disciplined spontaneous engagement. My surprising comment was anchored in an implicit assessment of the strength of Meg, and of our therapeutic alliance, and my sense of Meg's capacity to enter into a transitional creative space of virtual reality. The effect of the intervention was to provide a safe interval of some months for further exploratory work before the next crisis and self-destructive episode.

We consider this intervention from the vantage point of the analyst as a doer who potentially engages all seven motivational systems and, simultaneously, whose sense of self is actively implicated and affirmed in the process of empathic listening. This process can be affectively enlivening and lead to an increasingly confident, cohesive sense of self. Repetitive empathic listening can increase the subtle facets of the sense of self by contributing to a sense of satisfaction in establishing new paths for feeling "I am an analyst."

But, how did the analyst come up with the suggestion to Meg, "Do it now"? This was a novel, idiosyncratic suggestion, derived neither from any analytic theory nor from the analytic literature. To arrive at the "Do it now" intervention, we assume a rapid process of imaginative scanning took place. The analyst perused some "earmarked" items in Meg's history, as well as some items in the therapeutic relationship and also unidentified items in the analyst's own history. We propose the analyst's mind wandered briefly and rapidly to the tragic picture of Meg home alone cutting herself and then returned to mastering the complex task at hand with a spontaneous, nonreflective thought of "Do it here and I will be with you." In consequence both the analyst and Meg felt better connected to each other. Meg felt understood by him. And her analyst felt better. For the time being, a crisis had been averted as a result of a creative and surprisingly playful suggestion that the analyst's briefly wandering and semifocused or even unfocused mind had grasped.

The Distracted Mind or Mind Wandering Gone Awry

From a psychoanalytic perspective on development, we recognize that activities of a doer doing provide essential adaptive features that can coexist with or become a component of maladaptive patterns. In the following section we discuss how two adaptive developmental experiences – mind wandering and rough-and-tumble play – may play a role in ADD and ADHD. The evocative conjectures we present illustrate how new recognitions such as the importance in normal development of mind wandering and physically active play can help to explain familiar problematic occurrences in child and adult lived experiences.

When we refer to distraction we refer to the experience of being distracted from a task. To illustrate, a patient, Alan (treated by F. L) reported, among other difficulties, an extreme form of mind wandering. He is a 27-year-old photographer and photography student who is already enjoying some respect and recognition for his work. But, when he tries to read books on photography, or even look at photographs for more than a few minutes, his mind begins to wander. Before he knows it, he is reminiscing about last night's sexual encounter or previewing tonight's date. Often his mind wanders to a kaleidoscope of topics, tripping from one to another until he becomes aware of his "wandering mind" and forces himself to focus on the reading at hand. Prior to coming for therapy Alan had seen a psycho-pharmacologist who diagnosed attention deficit disorder and prescribed medication. Taking Ritalin helped for a while, but it turned out to be of limited benefit. He sought psychotherapy because he found himself procrastinating on his school assignments, though not his work assignments when he had a photography job. He admitted to being chronically sloppy which was amply confirmed by his outward appearance. Both the procrastination and sloppiness seemed to have been a consequence of his inattentiveness, his attention deficiency, and his wandering mind.

For Alan, analytic wisdom might indicate that conflicted sexual urges and fantasies are peremptorily pressing for attention and thereby interfering with nonsexual, exploratory activities. Psychoanalytic treatment would thus focus on exploring the sexual feelings and fantasies that intrude into his conscious attention and his nonsexual activities. His sexual conflicts could then be interpreted. Alan's sexual preoccupations are clearly motivated, but the kaleidoscope of thoughts that he also describes are reflective of "stimulus independent thoughts." In essence this is his mind "free associating" on its own. We will consider this mind wandering, taking our departure from a broader developmental perspective.

An essentially pathology-centered view that psychoanalysis and psychiatry hold with respect to lapses in attention, the ADD and ADHD diagnoses, can now be expanded by the research into the organization and adaptive function of the wandering mind. That is, the extent to which a person's mind wanders cannot be used to label this behavior as pathological per se, even though the person fails to retain an unswerving focus on a task at hand. Quo Vadis? Whither goeth thou, mind? All over the place, as the *self-sustaining* functions of the wandering mind have revealed.

As Alan's mind begins to wander on its own his accompanying experience, upon later reflection, is one of feeling compelled and somewhat out of control. Eventually he either tries to read his assignments again or goes to sleep, postponing his work to the next day. And to the next day, and so forth.

Although the two formulations of Alan's state of mind when he veers off task are compatible, there is an important difference between them. One formulation is that Alan's attention deficit is a consequence of intense sexual and aggressive conflicts that are spilling into his ability to pay attention and focus on cognitive and intellectual tasks. The alternative formulation has, so far, only been hinted at and not yet fully articulated. In broad strokes it can be stated that Alan's development veered him toward isolation in cognitive and intellectual pursuits and made learning experiences aversive and shame-laden. As a doer he found activities outside of his family from whom he wanted to distance himself while also craving their admiration. In his mind wandering he sought to find reinforcement for a cohesive sense of self. Is Alan best treated with a vantage point that sees the sexual fantasies, memories, and wishes as primary and contends that when he procrastinates he gives in to his pleasurable fantasies and masturbation? Or, is the more significant problem that Alan's excessive mind wandering is derived from early interferences in development? The sexual fantasies may then have been recruited to fill a developmental void. But, then again, why would this void be filled with sexual fantasies and masturbating? We will return to these questions later.

While explorations of conflictual issues are relevant, they do not address an important function of Alan's mind wandering. As we stated, a key aspect of mind wandering it that it engages our ability to be explicitly aware, or to become aware, of what we are currently feeling, sensing, thinking, and intending. Alan's awareness of his sexual reveries as he had them, and his rehearsals for the evening date, falls into this category. Precisely because of their strong affective presence, these thoughts required attention by managing past, and anticipating future, experiences. This was a formidable task for Alan as well as his area of vulnerability. To self-stabilize, or to prepare his sense of self, he needed to disengage his attention from whatever he perceived, or felt obliged to do, at that moment. This is what Alan describes as his inability to pay attention to what he reads as he reads.

When Alan was born, his parents were both physicians in their early 50s. He has an older brother and sister. Notable about his early life was the extent to which he had been left to his own devices. He recalled doing his school homework at the kitchen table while "a lot of family turmoil was going on all around. And all that was more interesting than the homework." When he needed help, his father would impatiently provide both criticism and answers.

Alan's parents were older than those of his classmates. His mother was apparently somewhat withdrawn and may have been suffering from a depression. His father was either negligibly involved with him or hypercritical. As interactive partners their contributions did not further Alan's ability to self-organize and work in a more focused manner.

Under favorable circumstances, student doers not only explore and gain knowledge but also reinforce and enliven their self-experience by engaging in the pleasurable task of learning. In the absence of this direct route to enhancing self-experience, mind wandering can fill in the void by reinforcing the sense of self. We propose that a strong tendency toward self-enhancement through mind wandering may become intractable and eventuate in a diagnosis of ADD or ADHD. Mind wandering – like fantasy – supplies a readily available nutrient to the sense of self and its repetitive addiction-like use provides temporary relief from shame, fear, and failure.

For Alan, patterns of learning were not established as a reliable background for task-focused learning. Furthermore, the task of focusing was embedded in an affectively highly arousing and distracting context. To focus required tuning out the "seductive" chaos around him. That proved to be difficult and somewhat risky. First, the task he felt he needed to focus on was gauging the extent of the family strife lest it become a danger to him. And furthermore, as Alan said, he was interested in observing the fights between his parents and between them and his sister.

Photography was a task in which he reigned supreme in the family. Its pursuit took him out of his home and into a novel world where he could be more active, a doer doing as he pleased. He preferred to take his camera into the streets rather than be cooped up in the family kitchen required to focus on schoolbooks, alone, in the midst of family chaos. No one in his family was particularly interested in photography, so this interest was entirely "his." He could master the process from beginning to end by doing it and now could gain satisfaction entirely through his own efforts.

Distractibility and difficulty in focusing have accompanied Alan since his early school days. Doing academic work increased his sense of incompetence. It contributed to his feeling ashamed, alone, and adrift within his family. The other family members seemed to cohere together while he felt like an outsider. In fact, a prominent theme of his photography projects, including a religious heritage project, was documenting "outsiders" in society. Alan's family was religious, and his first project in photography school was to document his religious heritage. That got his family's attention and even some respect.

118 The Wandering Mind

An ongoing theme in Alan's therapy was the extent to which he wanted to distinguish himself from his parents and siblings and yet be recognized and appreciated by them. He pretended not to be angry at their lack of appreciation of him.

As Alan and I investigated his life, we noted the split between his "sloppy" appearance, incomplete school assignments, and joyless days on the one hand, and his professional-appearing photography and active, rewarding sexual life on the other hand. In both of the latter he felt a sense of pride, competence, and pleasure. Furthermore, in photography and sexual activity he could focus and engage wholeheartedly. Alan was a large, almost obese, man in a family that was "trim." His appearance found favor with numerous girls as he grew up and enabled him to have a raucous sexual life. But, more intimate relationships were a problem. Although he prided himself on his sexual competence, keeping in mind that he had a partner could be difficult for him.

In the therapy sessions, his mind would wander to areas of competence and flit from situation to situation. As soon as it became clear to him that he was treading on thin ice – for example, nearing experiences that resembled his relationship with his father, such as being criticized for his sloppy appearance or messy apartment, with the implication that the other party "knew better" – he would scurry on to another thought.

The extent to which Alan could share his experience with me was particularly crucial in his treatment. In speaking about his sexual exploits, he would begin to veer away from discussing those recollections in which he was viewed as having been insensitive to the feelings of his partner. During intimate moments, his mind wandering and his "distraction" would prompt a girlfriend to feel ashamed, hurt, and angry, and to end their relationship. We could link Alan's behavior to his experiences of criticism and shaming in his family.

The ADD in Alan's case was a disorder of self-regulation in the context of either absent or aversive interactive regulation. Abandoned to his own devices, Alan sought ways to find an accepting home with his family that provided him with some sense of competence and esteem. As a photographer he could both stand outside his photographs as an observer but also feel himself into the pictures of the struggling outsiders. As a sexual performer (doer) in his sexual life he remained engaged, while as a responder and relater to his partner he reverted to his outsider status.

Being an outsider provided Alan with a compromise that allowed him to feel being a part of his family while offering both some protection against their criticism for his academic failings and some insulation from his father's professed superiority in all matters. The distractibility and inability to focus were the consequences

The Wandering Mind   119

of failures to engage "academic" processes in an interactive context that could offer the joy of learning, provide some balanced sense of tolerable excitement and calm, as well as offer an organization, a scaffold for future learning experiences.

What might have provided Alan with a container or scaffold for his excessively wandering mind? How did Alan compensate, or try to compensate, for the missing experiences that might have provided earlier organization and coherence to his sense of self? Based on mind wandering research, our proposal is that for traumatized people like Alan and many others ADD is both a symptom and an attempt at self-cure aimed at reinforcing the sense of self through mind wandering.

For the past two decades the diagnoses Attention Deficit Disorder and Attention Deficit Hyperactivity Disorder have become a catchall for a variety of symptoms and behavioral problems in children. Since its first usage, the children so diagnosed have by now become adults as had Alan. But rather than being arrived at through the experience and reports of the afflicted person, child or adult, these diagnostic categories are based on the observations of school personnel, therapists, and other adults.

Children diagnosed with ADHD are generally unable to behave themselves according to school requirements. Their ability to focus attention is limited. Like Alan, they veer into play or daydreaming at the expense of focusing on school assignments. Like Alan, but only to a limited degree, the wandering of ADD children is not in the mind but appears in physical activities. Thus they become disruptive in the classroom. In adulthood they may seek work that enables them to move about a great deal and even when more sedentary tasks are required, they find themselves playing Internet games or fidgeting.

Children diagnosed as ADHD are often lost in their own daydreams and thus make only fleeting contact with other children, adults, or therapists. Or, like Marco, who will be described below, they run about, flitting from item to item, unable to attend to a task. The upshot is that the ADHD diagnosis covers a broad spectrum of difficulties and can result in considerable misunderstanding and pathologizing of those who have been so labeled.

In psychotherapy with children diagnosed as ADHD, Eva-Maria Topel (Topel, 2004; Topel & Lachmann, 2007) often finds a severely depressed, or withdrawn, mother or father in the background. Topel is a psychologist and psychotherapist who treats children, adolescents, and families in Neureichenau, Germany. The affect disorders of the parents, according to Topel, tend to be unrecognized and therefore remained untreated. Through their hyperactivity these children can be understood to be coercing or trying to arouse their frightened and frightening withdrawn parents (Lyon-Ruth, 2003) to become more alive and more related. Topel emphasizes the contribution of the parents to their children's hyperactive reaction. Along with mind wandering, associated hyperactivity of the child may also be an attempt at self-cure. Topel has argued that, at an enormous cost to their lives, some of these children may also be trying to "cure their parents" (Miller, 1981).

Of course, we can ask, did the parents withdraw because of their frustration and inability to cope with their children? That could set off a vicious cycle of hyperactivity in the child that would lead to the parents' increasing withdrawal, which in turn would lead back again to the child's increased hyperactivity. Or, are both parent and child "victims" of a larger, general societal trend that for some children goes counter to their developmental requirements? To address this latter position we turn to the work of Jaak Panksepp (1998).

Through his groundbreaking studies of emotions in humans and animals, Panksepp has addressed the increasing frequency of the ADHD diagnosis in many cultures. Based on his studies of developmental necessities in young animals – baby rats, for example – Panksepp has delineated the crucial role of rough-and-tumble play in promoting social relationships. In male and female animals, lively physical play is usually initiated by the mother through poking and tickling her baby. The play then expands from the mother to siblings and other animals. Later, the father may participate but usually not with as light a touch as the mother. Whereas his style may differ from the mother's, his participation enlarges the experience and the fun for his offspring. Panksepp notes that when baby animals are prevented from engaging in rough-and-tumble play at the developmentally appropriate time, approximately 13 days after birth for rats, then, when they do have the opportunity for rough-and-tumble play, they pursue it with increased vigor and vehemence. To Panksepp this means that the activity itself is not based on prior learning, since that has not taken place. Rather it is based on a neurological/developmental necessity. In translating his findings to humans, Panksepp argues for the importance of play, specifically rough-and-tumble play, in development.

Now comes the important leap. To the extent that rough-and-tumble play – physical contact, pushing and jumping on another child and playfully pinning him down on the ground – has been discouraged in schools and homes, then to that extent the need for playfulness continues and in Panksepp's proposal emerges as ADHD: excessive mind wandering combined with hyperactivity. Panksepp refers to children with ADHD as "excessively playful children" (p. 320). He asks, "Are they now being medicated to reduce their natural desire to play, on the pretext that they have some type of impulse-control disorder? . . . If so, it seems necessary to provide them substantial opportunities for rough and tumble play at the appropriate time of day, such as early in the morning when such urges are especially high" (p. 320).

We propose that the value of the wandering mind and the necessity for rough-and-tumble play in children establishes an early balance between predominantly mental and predominantly physical activities. These two activities are prominent in childhood behavior disturbances, where the child withdraws and is lost in a world of daydreams at one extreme and in hyperactive, totally absorbing play and bodily activities at the other extreme. The ADD and ADHD diagnoses span this entire range.

Working with Alan was similar to working with any other adult patient. But treating a child diagnosed as ADHD can indeed be strenuous and exhausting. Quite quickly one's office can look as though a whirlwind has swirled through it. The therapist may feel especially sympathetic toward the parents who have to deal with this child on a daily basis. Why teachers and parents should feel helpless and depressed, overburdened and angry when trying to teach or train, calm, or focus such a child becomes eminently understandable.

When a child or adult carrying a diagnosis of ADHD enters psychotherapy, the problems in affect regulation and the limitation this difficulty imposes on their emotional life quickly become apparent. When parents withdraw, criticize, and punish their children's lively behavior, the children become the solitary victims of their unmanageable feelings of anger and emptiness. Often isolated from other family members and left to their own devices, they cannot develop the resources to engage others in a reciprocal affective responsiveness. Reciprocal engagements with others are precisely what Panksepp states are a benefit of engaging in rough-and-tumble play. Thus, the dearth of the children's social skills and resources further distances them from others and establishes the vicious cycle we have described.

The Treatment of Marco: ADHD in a Child

Just before he was 4 years old, Marco arrived at my (treated by E.-M. Topel) office with his parents, and I heard him yelling and stomping around outside my office. When I appeared, he first ran toward then away from my entrance door. His parents reluctantly ran after him and tried to catch him and calm him down. They even attempted to reason with him as they tried to catch him, but to no avail. They muttered an apologetic "Hello" in my direction, while Marco literally bumped into me. He bounced off me and shouted some words I could not understand. I opened the door to my office and Marco dashed into the room. This frenetic activity may have been Marco's improvised version of rough-and-tumble play. None of us were aware of this possibility at the time. Understandably,

Marco had no playmates. I realized that Marco's attachment style was avoidant and that prompted me to turn away from him rather than activate his turning away from me.

Once in my office, Marco stood motionlessly, and appeared to be amazed. He then ran from one side of the office to the other, shouting questions, such as, "What is this? What is that?" He did not wait for an answer.

I indicated to Marco's parents where in my office they might sit and I sat down. I watched Marco silently and asked myself whether he would "check" with me (Topel & Lachmann, 2007). That is, would he try to see what I was doing or not doing? Was I OK with what he was doing or not doing? What can he anticipate from me? So, with my body slightly averted, without looking at him directly, I waited for him to take the initiative in establishing some contact with me. I did not want to add to his experience of feeling forced to comply with a demand to "relate" and thus place him in a position either to "accommodate" (Brandchaft et al., 2010) or, more likely, to rebel or defy. In either case he might then feel even more isolated and alone.

Waiting for Marco to take the first step in establishing a relationship with me was my attempt to convey to him that I understood his need to feel safe, unpressured, and respected, as well as his uncontrollable need to move his body about. I was protecting his sense of agency as central to his identity and need to feel safe. My intent was not to interfere with his need to be a doer doing in the only way he could express his need to be active. At the same time I became aware of his parents' growing nervousness. Perhaps they were not used to someone responding to Marco's "lack of cooperation" with an adult authority. I signaled to them by smiling to indicate that I knew what I was doing and hoped that they might be able to relax, wait, and wonder. Out of the corner of my eye I noticed that Marco actually did check out my face for a second as he ran around the room shouting his questions. Marco was testing me to see if he was really safe and, if so, he would eventually relax.

So, how could I get Marco's attention? I planned a sequence of behaviors with Marco, beginning with parallel speech. It entails both of us speaking at the same time but not to each other. Parallel speech is not interactive speech. It could enable Marco to remain detached and simultaneously establish some contact with me. It serves as a way of unobtrusively accompanying a child as he or she moves through a rapidly changing world. It offers a confirmation: "You are not alone; somebody is here who hears you and watches what you are doing." Accompanying Marco in this way, I let my mind wander, and mused out loud (Lachmann, 2000). I talked as though I was just talking to myself as I watched him "fly" around the room touching this and that item. Marco flying around the room was a physical action parallel to a mind flitting from one subject to the next. Marco did not have or had not yet developed the resources to activate his mind and needed his whole being, physically, to simulate this activity.

As Marco ran about the room, I said, "Hum, what might this be? What might that be for?" Marco stopped uttering words that had no meaning to me, but he did continue to touch things. My intervention, paralleling my comments with his activities, paved the way for an experience of shared direction. My mind wandering, loosely, accompanied Marco in his active, physical wanderings.

In the sessions I provided for Marco the basic interactive experiences that parents intuitively use when communicating with their babies. These experiences provide their child with the experience of an interacting partner and accrue to a sense of self and self-with-other (Stern, 1985). At one point Marco touched a toy sword, cautiously, and as I tried to catch him, I said to him: "Oh, a sword . . . for a knight?" Marco looked at me. At that point I shifted from loose mind wandering to engaging my mind in a task, a narration. Marco was thereby provided with a greater degree of agency through a more coherent narrative task. He could thereby derive a more coherent, organized sense of agency using the knight I introduced into his "story."

I felt affirmed in my approach and continued: "What story might be connected to the sword?" Marco took the sword, and waved it wildly toward his father. Marco's father seemed to be prepared to ward off one of his son's quite dangerous appearing advances. That is, he rapidly interpreted the situation in probably his customary and concrete manner.

I thought that the father-son relationship did not include rough-and-tumble role-playing and pretend play. I asked the father if he could just play with Marco. Could he be a storyteller? Could he imagine a story about knights and swords? He required some coaching from me before he was able to do so. Nevertheless he continued to glance at me doubtfully as he tried to play with Marco.

Marco calmed down, listened, and became engaged in the story. From time to time he waved his sword, but he was soon sitting on his father's lap. At the end of this first session, the whole family left. They appeared to be livelier than when they had come in. This was true even for the mother who barely participated. Marco asked why the time was over already. I thought that boded well for the future of his treatment.

Marco's History

Marco's mother was in her mid-40s when Marco, her third child, was born. She had two children from a previous marriage. Marco's father was nearly 60. I was

124 The Wandering Mind

told by both parents that they initially felt ambivalent about having a child. "But," said his mother, "when I saw him, I knew at once, he was the child I had been waiting for." She did not know why. For her, Marco was a wanted child. However, difficulties began quite early for mother and baby. During breast feeding Marco turned his face away from her and cried for hours. She could not calm him down. I could imagine how disappointed Marco's mother had felt. Her expectations of Marco were dashed. Even before the pediatrician entered the scene Marco was establishing an avoidant attachment.

Marco's father wanted a quiet home and the mother felt that he reproached her for having a baby so late in their lives. Arguments ensued and soon all three were crying. Marco was taken to a pediatrician who diagnosed "an inherent tendency for ADHD" and prescribed medication. Marco was medicated and then slept longer in the morning. However, during feedings he would often appear drowsy. Soon, his temper tantrums appeared. The pediatrician now advised them to medicate him consistently and to be firm in demanding that Marco eat and sleep at appropriate times.

When Marco was 3 years old his parents tried to place him in a daycare program. He was rejected and labeled "too difficult, too aggressive, and unable to wait and to regulate himself in a group." Marco behaved strikingly like those baby animals in Panksepp's study who, having been deprived of rough-and-tumble play at their appropriate developmental time, behaved increasingly aggressively. Asked about Marco's early development, his mother recalled that when she fed him, she would not give in to his "little quirks." Marco wanted to eat little portions all day long. She felt that in this way Marco wanted to control her. Her eyes narrowed as she told me this, and she added that he gave her back very little for her love. A vicious circle of "chase and dodge" (Beebe & Lachmann, 2002) had been established, with the mother demanding that he eat according to her expectations, and Marco dodging, turning away from her body and her face. Marco's parents tried to follow a regimen to raise him by providing the firm "boundaries" and "conventional temporal rhythms" that the pediatrician and others whom they had consulted had prescribed. Sadly, Marco's noncompliant responses made his mother feel like a failure. She became angry, and her anger showed in her face as she interacted with Marco. It seemed to me that Marco, upon sensing his mother's anger and seeing her angry face, become increasingly affectively and cognitively dysregulated. Marco's father stayed out of these daily dramas. In retrospect, we believe, the advice that Marco be given firm boundaries, and that he be expected to eat and sleep at appropriate, conventional times may have exacerbated his symptomatic behavior. In Louis Sander's (1977) study comparing newborns who received mutually regulated, on-demand feeding with newborns who were fed according to a schedule, the babies fed on demand quite quickly developed normal wake-sleep cycles compared to the babies who were fed according to a schedule. In Marco's development the attempt to impose conventional eating and sleeping patterns may have interfered with the establishment of natural hunger and sleep rhythms. Marco turning his head away during his mother's attempts to feed him may have been his signal to her that she was interfering in his establishing regulatory control of hunger needs rather than a specific aversive reaction to his mother, which was how she misread it. Certainly after her continuous efforts, Marco's turning his head away became an expression of aversion as well. However, initially, Marco may simply have been conveying "not now."

Imposing conventional eating and sleeping times on Marco may well have resulted in increasing his defiance and sense of alienation from his family thus increasing his aggressive, hyperactive behavior. Like Alan, Marco was pointed in the direction of increased solitary self-regulation in the face of unresponsive and unreliable interactive regulation. In both instances the child was not prepared to manage such extensive self-regulation on his own.

Regulating physiological needs became a solitary activity for both Alan and Marco. For Marco it occurred in defiance of his mother. From this vantage point Marco's hyperactivity was a self-assertive response to feeling that his bodily rhythms were being undermined by having conventions imposed on him that went counter to his natural bodily rhythms. For Alan, self-regulation included mind wandering and a heightened focus on his sexuality. In the treatment of both Alan and Marco, accompanying them in their self-regulation, a form of interactive regulation, decreased their sense of aloneness or, put differently, promoted patterns of self-regulation in an interactively regulating context.

The treatments of both Marco and Alan illustrate that what appeared to be ADD and ADHD can be understood and treated as disorders in self-regulation and interactive regulation (Beebe & Lachmann, 2002). Marco brought to the interaction a hypersensitivity and particular difficulties in physiological regulation that in interactions with his mother led to dysregulated temporal rhythms. With failed interactive regulation, Marco was increasingly left on his own, and to his own self-regulatory efforts. His hyperactivity, his need to keep "running," was an attempt to provide some physical regulation in the absence of having it provided in a contingent manner by either parent. The medication he was given may have provided him with some temporary calming but failed to address his need for physiological regulation and thus proved to be not only inadequate but also counterproductive.

126 The Wandering Mind

Recall the question we posed earlier: Was Alan's concentration problem primarily the result of sexual fantasies and wishes, and his problem with procrastination the result of his giving in to his pleasurable fantasies and masturbating? Or, was the primary problem Alan's excessive mind wandering derived from early interferences in development, with his sexual fantasying and masturbation secondary to filling in the void? In response we bring together the researches on the wandering mind and rough-and-tumble play. We propose that rough-and-tumble play fulfills two functions simultaneously. One, described by Panksepp, is the opportunity to engage in interactive socializations that prepare and promote peer relations and help to establish one's presence in the world at large. For both young animals and humans this entails increasing one's sense of competence, safety, and security in the world and, conversely, decreasing one's feeling of danger. But, we propose a second benefit, at least for children. Rough-and-tumble play energizes one's feeling of contact with one's own extremities and one's entire body. It embeds, connects, and integrates the sense of self in one's bodily experience and establishes or furthers a familiarity with one's feeling of being in one's body. These feelings are the scaffold that provides the wandering mind with an implicit terrain, a home in which the mind wandering can live.

The function of mind wandering within a bodily embedded sense of self is different from the necessity to find compensations for an impaired sense of self in which the mind wandering is uncontrolled. In masturbating Alan relied on implicitly reinforcing his sense of self in a way that had become prominent during puberty. At that time he was already much larger than his schoolmates, which curtailed "rough-and-tumble" activities with other boys. In Alan's case, masturbation served as a self-affirming function. It connected him with his body, his entire body, as no other experiences of his life did. My dialogue with Alan focused on the self-sustaining aspects of his symptomatology. As Alan's sense of self became more articulated in therapy his distractibility decreased. Simultaneously, mind wandering gradually assumed a place in his life that was more consistent with its normal "hygienic" functions.

Summary

In this essay we have focused on two aspects of the early formation of the doer doing – that is, of an enlivened sense of self. The activity of mind wandering activates and reinforces a sense of self-organization and self-coherence while simultaneously covering a breadth of experiences that contain memories and aspects of being a doer doing with others and with oneself. The wandering mind sweeps up these experiences and organizes them in images, thoughts, feelings, actions, intentions, and goals in ways that make them "our own." Bodily experiences like rough-and-tumble play, which entails a particularly enlivening sense of doer doing, contribute to delineating a bodily sense of self. These experiences of later childhood are in continuity with the earlier self and self-with-other touch, tickle, toss, and "gotcha" games of the first year. The two sources, the mental activity that makes for mind wandering as a constituent of the sense of self and the physical activity that involves feeling the contours and connections to all parts of one's body reinforce each other. In the absence of a firm sense of self as a doer doing, of experiencing physical and mental initiating and responding, and having one's initiative responded to, the person, child, or adult seeks compensatory activities that will reinforce body awareness and body boundaries as well as a sense of ownership and familiarity with one's body. Marco's running about and Alan's masturbating fulfilled these functions.

Self-expression and self-recognition are closely related. The better we actualize ourselves in our actions, the better we feel we know ourselves and are known by others. The principal function of mind wandering is the daily repetitive connecting with one's self, one's intentions, goals, and mind states, over and over. A mother's talk patterns are an important model for mind wandering in her baby, who does in behavior what the mother has been conveying in words. The baby's actions are a parallel language to the mother's words. In the treatment of Marco, the therapist had to reverse this process by enabling Marco to connect with words that paralleled his actions. In the treatment of Alan, a variant of this process also applied. For him a disconnection between action and words eventuated in his reviving actions to supplement the extent to which words did not sufficiently reinforce his sense of self. Both Marco and Alan devoted their time to variants of rough-and-tumble play to supplement their difficulty in sustaining a sense of self. Although Alan engaged in considerable mind wandering, it was burdened by his ever-present, shame-loaded recognition that he was failing to perform much needed tasks. With his childhood deficit in having his intellectual development supported he could not derive the satisfaction that mind wandering unburdened by shame can provide. In both illustrations, we can recognize the need for motor activity from birth on as a crucial, parallel, and interrelated development for both the mind at a task and the wandering mind.

Coda

We regard our proposals in this book as part of a larger ongoing project carried forward in our joint and individual books and papers. Our approach to mind, like Freud's in regard to instinctual drive, begins with an account of motivation. Unlike Freud, who relied on notions of psychic structures and instinctual energies, we have used nonlinear systems as our container concept. By motivation we refer to the experiences of an affect, intention, and goal with an emphasis on experience as it is lived – that is, with much of it in full awareness and much of it not. Eschewing a view of the mind as separated into structures, we emphasize the unity of "self," meaning an integrated sense of self, an experiential self that retains a sense of continuity over changing epochs of life and despite the constant moment-to-moment shift of emotions, intentions, and goals. To draw out our proposals we have searched for confirmations between clinical experience, developmental research and observation, and the findings of neuroscience.

In this book we have tried to make three particular contributions to psychoanalytic practice and theory. In our initial essay, we explored research and observations on the first year of life. These findings provided support for our hypothesis that being a doer doing, initiating and responding, is the origin of the enlivenment of a sense of self that encompasses living in one's body and the surrounding world of animate others and inanimate objects. We have drawn on infant studies to propose 12 qualities and capacities that arise in the first year and are critical for the richness of subsequent development.

In our middle essay we presented two clinical experiences that stand on their own as additional examples of the application of motivational systems theory and the therapeutic approaches we have previously described. Here we added comments that integrate the clinical stories with our emphasis on the significance of the 12 qualities and capacities originating in the first year. We believe these qualities and capacities have application for understanding the dynamics of any clinical experience.

In this last essay, we have highlighted the enlivening of the sense of self derived from mind wandering. By mind wandering we refer to the experience of loose rambling thoughts and feelings that occur spontaneously when a person is not engaged in a purposeful activity and goal. We have argued that an animated experience of agency is not restricted to occasions when a person is being a doer doing with a task-centered definitive goal. An additionally important goal is to be maximally in touch with one's immediate mind state, one's here-and-now preoccupations with relationships and intentions – and that is what is accomplished by the wandering mind. Using spontaneous mind wandering as a starting point, we have explored other experientially similar mind states, both adaptive and maladaptive.

The history of psychoanalysis reveals many attempts by different theorists to single out one factor as "the" or "the most" significant aspect of development, psychopathology, or therapeutic action. Examples are theorists who cite intrapsychic conflict as central and others who cite relational interactions. Our approach is and has been to seek a balanced view over several critical explanatory domains.

In prior writings we have sought a balanced view of motivational systems – citing seven different systems – each of which may be dominant at any moment or period of time individually or in combination. Now we sought a further balance – between the enlivenment derived from the focused activation of intentions and goals of a motivational system and the additional enlivenment of mind wandering.

In all three essays we have tried to emphasize the significance of continuity of experience of the sense of self that enlivens the feeling of an individual identity and personhood. We attempted to place that continuity within a developmental perspective focused on emergence and change in a way that can be adapted to an exploration of the mutative factors in treatment. We have also tried to give a balanced picture of implicit factors affecting lived experience, citing a background "hum" accompanying the doer doing in each motivational system. Then, too, we have tried to take cognizance of the many aspects of nonconscious processes while simultaneously recognizing the unique human propensity to form imagistic and verbal narratives – stories that give organization to our lived experiences.

Throughout we have tried to recognize the distinction between an experiential and process accounting of a sense of self. From an experiential point of view we can feel ourselves to be highly individualistic both while asserting our preferences and in our responses to our own bodies, while, at other times, we feel ourselves deeply embedded in attachment and affiliative relationships. From a process perspective, we are never a psychologically separate entity, never an isolated mind, but always exist in a field of multiple contingent influences. In our account of therapeutic action we balance the beneficial effect of the search for insight and meaning through interpretation and shared inquiry, and the more implicit effect of multiple relational factors affecting thresholds for activating emotions, trust, safety, and cooperation. Even more generally we have attempted to offer a balanced view of adaptive and maladaptive development emphasizing qualities and capacities that propel forward an enlivened sense of self. We have attempted to advance theories that strike a balanced view of explanations of "normal," healthy, adaptive development, and explanations of maladaptive developmental trends and psychopathology.

Afterword
Toward a Metatheory – a Diagrammatic Portrayal

In *Psychoanalysis and Motivational Systems: A New Look* (Lichtenberg et al., 2011) we presented three diagrams that illustrated our view of the functioning of the psyche with special attention to motivational systems. Here we will re-present the three diagrams and text with slight modifications and then add a fourth and fifth diagram. Through the five diagrams and explanatory text we hope to present a broad integrative theory of mind, a metatheory with a particular emphasis on motivation (affects, intentions, and goals) and fluctuations in the sense of self.

The original three diagrams indicate how we view the working of each individual mind (diagram 1), the dyadic experience of comparably functioning individuals (diagram 2), and the dyadic experience of an asymmetrical pair such as adult and child (diagram 3). Similar diagrams could be added to portray the interactions of motivational systems in groups of larger size or more varied composition. Taken as a whole, the three diagrams were intended to illustrate the varieties of mental functioning and experiences that emerge from seven distinct but interrelated motivational systems. Our idea is that at any moment an individual may be focused on a task relevant to one or more intentions or goals. In a symmetrical or asymmetrical dyad, the pair may or may not share a focus on the same or comparable intentions. Our prior emphasis was on individuals doing and responding via an active task-centered focus on a goal. The goal could be to achieve physiological regulation; or to experience an attachment connection; or offer caregiving; or form an affiliative link to a group; or to indicate aversion; or explore the inner, outer, and shared world and assert one's own preferences; or to experience sensual and/ or sexual enjoyment and arousal. In other words, while focused on distinct motivational systems, in focusing on a common task between the members of the dyad, we were concerned to portray motivational systems in an intersubjective context.

In this Afterword, we reprise these original three diagrams while adding a new one, diagram 4. As before, our intention is to define a task and a pattern (or system) designed to accomplish this task and thus achieve a motivational goal in an intersubjective context. Our overall view is that systems of affects, intentions, and goals self-organize, self-stabilize, and exist in a state of tension of increasing complexity from early infancy on. When activated, each motivational system works toward adaptation to the exigencies arising from the infant being in an expanding world as a doer doing. At any age, as individuals attempt to achieve the goal of an intention, they work to improve efficacy, learn to predict their own doings and the doings of involved others, and gain satisfaction and confidence. This complex effort to follow an intention, learn in the course of the doing, gain efficacy, negotiate difficulties, make adjustments, and gain satisfaction and confidence is symbolized by the arrows in each motivational system (or branch) in diagram 4.

Diagram 1 is our attempt to portray the mind of an individual as he or she attempts to achieve effectiveness, safety, and satisfaction as a doer doing in the world.

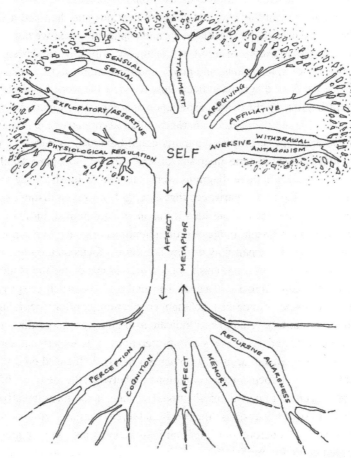

Diagram 1 A doer doing.

Schematically, each root of the tree refers to the systems that are the foundation of all human mental functioning – perception, cognition, memory, affect, and recursive awareness. The functioning of these five foundational systems is generally described separately. In contrast, we wish to highlight the idea that their integrated provision of information is crucial for the effective realization of the goals of each motivational system. The trunk thus represents a dual pathway for information about the external and internal world and knowledge of success and failure in initiating and carrying forward intentions and goals. Arrows pointing up could indicate information that has emerged from the foundational systems to cue and inform the motivational systems. Arrows pointing down could represent a pathway for knowledge gained from the activity of any activated motivational system. But here the complexity of lived experience easily escapes the limits of a schematic drawing. For example, a young man unexpectedly sees a young woman he is infatuated with in a movie line. He experiences a confusion of perceptions: Is it really her? Then a stream of thoughts: She looks great. And memories: Our last date ended awkwardly. And affects: surprise, excitement, then apprehension about her reception of him. All this would be represented by up arrows. As he approaches and talks to her (activating his attachment and sensual motivational systems), he makes adjustments as he learns about the likely success or failure of his intentions from her reception of his initiatives and how well his being a doer doing matches that of hers. This knowledge (which would be represented by arrows going down) then influences his perceptions and his mode of thinking about himself and her. The result of the circularity is the emergence of old and recent memories, the expansion of his range of emotion, and an increase in his knowledge of himself in a romance. In an oversimplication in diagram 1 we singled out metaphor and affect as the principal "carriers" of the messages up and down. By affect, we mean feelings, emotions, sensations, and sensibilities at all levels of implicit and explicit awareness. By metaphor, we refer to linkages between subsymbolic, imagistic symbolic, and verbal symbolic encodings of information.

Each of the seven tree limbs represents a motivational system. The arrows back and forth along the limbs in diagram 4 indicate the pursuit of intentions and goals and the attempt to work toward efficacy and competence. In the center we place the sense of self. We regard the sense of self as an emergent quality of an individual being a doer doing, initiating and responding, activating and downregulating. All of this activity, by which the self enlivens itself, is framed and channeled through the motivational systems.

Why a tree? We used a tree to evoke the repetitive pattern of fractals found across all nature and proposed an analogy between nature-based fractals and the repetitive patterns of lived experience. Selfsameness of repetition across

134 Afterword

dimensions of scale and time helps to account for the relative stability of the sense of self, of human identity and personhood, despite continuous change in mental states and epochs of life. We draw on an analogy between motivational systems and the tree as a commonly used example of a fractal based on the repetitive invariant self-similarity of roots, limbs, and branches. In a tree, the same pattern is used over and over again as the tree grows, resulting in structures that ultimately vary in size and location, but remain essentially similar and integrated. For us, the limbs and their branches in our diagrams represent the seven motivational systems, and the roots represent the foundational subsystems of perception, cognition, memory, affects, and recursive awareness. Both the foundational subsystems and the motivational systems are constructed using the same basic informational circuits, which vary in terms of their intensity, their activation over time, and their comprehensiveness. Consider the following: An intuition can be tributary to an inkling, and an inkling can be tributary to a fancy, which can lead to a pretty clear intention and thence to a commitment. Similarly an almost reflex-like wink can lead to heavens knows what. In analysis we sometimes deal with repetition compulsions, which can be thought of as maladaptive sequences and patterns that get bigger, more intense, and more comprehensive, rather than shriveling up, in the face of failure. These are all fractal structures, whether adaptive or maladaptive, and they allow a sense of self-continuity and enlivenment across a range of intensity, duration, and scope of motivational activations. Another fractal-like invariant similarity is that each motivational system repetitively receives information processed by the same foundational systems, and each foundational system receives information from the activity of an activated motivational system. In our diagrams, communication between the foundational subsystems and the motivational systems (between the roots and limbs) is represented by the trunk, which has a continual circular flow of affects, metaphoric processes, and much more. But the static two dimensions of the diagrams give a false impression of a linear sequence. Ideally the diagrams would have the full three dimensions of a tree. Then each foundation system (root) would be equidistant from the others, conveying the interplay and mutual influence of their functioning. And each motivational system (branch) would be equidistant from the others, conveying equal potential for one group of affects, intentions, and goals to shift and flow into another. Better still would be a three-dimensional model in time, say as captured by video screen.

Diagrams 2 and 3 represent intersubjectivity and dyadic intimacy. The limbs and branches of each tree leaning toward the other represent the interactions and bidirectional mutual influences of a dyad. Diagram 2 portrays the interaction of

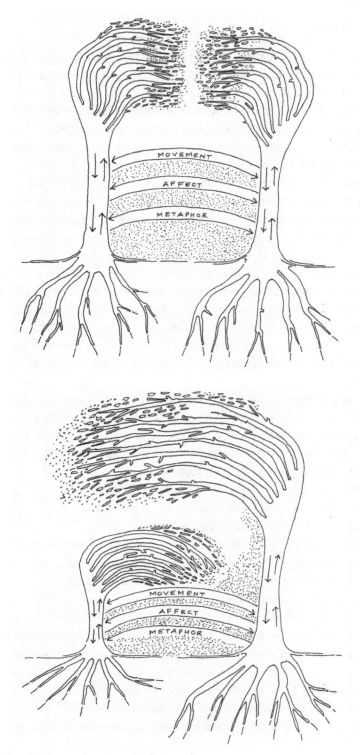

Diagrams 2 and 3 Doers doing in a dyadic interchange.

motivational systems between a more or less symmetrical pair: analyst and analysand, a married couple, close friends, and colleagues. Diagram 3 portrays the interaction of motivational systems between a more or less asymmetrical pair: parent and child, student and teacher. The actual situation, while still being assymetrical, could be just as partial, or complex, or even fraught, as what we might find with a symmetrical pair. As every infant learns, smiles that worked very well in the morning sometimes no longer carry the day when it is time to go to bed. In terms of the diagrams, the bidirectional arrows between the trunks of the trees that indicate movement (behavior), affects, and metaphor (implicit and explicit informational exchanges) represent communication and mutual regulation. For its part, the shaded area between the two trees represents the emotional ambience and the realm of implicit knowing of the other that the dyad has cocreated.

To be noted, in diagram 3, which represents an asymmetrical pair, the arrows connoting communication of movement and affect are bidirectional, while the informational exchange indicated by verbal metaphor is unidirectional. (The shaded area once again represents the considerable significance of the cocreated affective domain, the implicit relational knowing, that exists between caregiver and child.) Even at an early age the bidirectional sensitivity to movement and emotion is more or less equivalent – this is one of the great surprises of detailed mother-infant observational studies – while metaphor moves more from parent to child. In the realm of fantasy and unconscious imagistic symbolization, any of the diagrams, whether the single tree, the more or less symmetrical dyad, or the asymmetrical dyad, may be representative of the patient's or analyst's *conception* of what is taking place on the therapeutic stage.

Another dimension of fractals that is relevant in our analogy is the openness of their boundaries and the dynamic transactional potential invited by that openness of boundaries. A cloud can be viewed as enclosed within its boundaries. However, since the boundaries both enclose and are open, the openness makes it possible for one cloud to merge effortlessly with another or separate into parts, all from the perspective of the viewer. To be sure, with a tree, the analogy is only approximate though serviceable: We can think of the leafy canopy as more or less continuous, as a boundary that, for example, can keep out sunlight and even rain, while up close, we encounter openness between the various elements – that is, leaves, twigs, and small branches – that actually comprise the crown. Viewed up close, the boundary is open. And in fact, leaves, twigs, and small branches originating from another sizeable limb may be found infiltrating the open spaces in their own quest for sunlight.

In our view, the qualities of enclosure/container and boundary openness apply to each motivational system and, more importantly, to the relationship of each system

Afterword 137

to each of the others. We view each system as an enclosure for one grouping of self-similar affects, intentions, and goals. For example, the attachment system "contains" positive feelings associated with an intention to form a safe intimate relationship with another. Yet, at the boundary, an attachment may take on a negative quality, merging with and then shifting to the aversive system, or a sensual quality, merging with and then shifting to the sensual/sexual system, or a concern for the well-being of the other, merging with and shifting over to the caregiving system.

We believe this dimension of fractals – the openness to smooth transactions at the boundary – explains the seamless shift from dominance by one motivational system to dominance by another. In comparison to the quality of openness, the contrasting quality of fractals and goals having boundaries is not so much represented by the boundary of the canopy – as analysts we know how porous boundaries can be – as by the unique combination of both motives and foundational system as they come together in the trunk. This is what is experienced by the individual as a unique sense of self, as one who functions autonomously despite being embedded in an intersubjective matrix. No, what the open nature of fractal boundaries in the canopy best captures is the experience of the self entering the state of mind of another or merged with the other. Further, in our view, fractal theory also applies to the flow of psychic contents as well as to the output of the systems that are foundational to their emergence. For example, self-similar themes repeat and repeat across the dimension of time – sometimes as a major dynamic of a session or a week's sessions, sometimes as a major dynamically laden, yet fleeting, association in a session.

Features that are central to one motivational system can readily play a part in the functioning of other systems. Sharing of common features by several motivational systems contributes to the sense of continuity during shifts in mental states. Interest, and affects central to the exploratory motivational system, for example, can activate curiosity associated with intentions that unfold in any of the other systems. Similarly, efficacy and competence, the core goals of the exploratory system, can easily be included in the goals of the other systems. Cooperation, an evolutionary contribution central to the attachment, affiliative, and caregiving systems, is a valuable feature of the other systems. A sense of safety, a core aspect of attachment, is likewise a feature underlying optimal functioning of the other systems. Frustration, a hallmark of activation of the aversive system, may arise in any of the other systems, where it may be resolved without a shift in state or, as often happens, may result in a brief or lasting shift to the aversive system. Sensual pleasure, essential to the sensual/sexual system, is also essential to the attachment and caregiving systems, and as well is commonly a feature of affiliation and physiological activities, such as eating, sleeping, urinating, and defecating. Excitement, central to the orgiastic goal of sexuality, may occur in any system and may be incorporated into the aversive system in power-centered domination/submission fantasies and activities. Bodily awareness, central to physiological regulation, has an omnipresent potential for "messaging" into the activity of any system, especially in activity that involves motility, strenuous exertion, and changes in equilibrium. Language and all conscious and unconscious cognition expressive of the intentions and goals of every system are accordingly saturated with "body-speak" as a metaphoric link between physiologically centered and other mental states.

Diagrams 4 and 5 illustrate the view of the "tree" from the top. While diagram 4 illustrates the complex affective and cognitive challenges faced by the doer doing when focused on a task, diagram 5 portrays the "wandering mind." We can think of the wandering mind as the nontask mind to contrast it with the intentions and goals delineated in fully activated motivational systems. While the experience of one's mind focused on a task defined by a motivational goal and one's mind wandering is distinctly different, the implication that the wandering mind (or misnamed "mind at rest" or "default position") is without a significant human goal is grossly inaccurate. As illustrated in the wandering mind diagram (diagram 5), the center of the tree where the limbs come together symbolizes the "I," the me, the person and all his or her preoccupations in the form of loose associations to the lived experience of daily life intentions in the now moment. In mind wandering, this sense of "I" potentially includes associative links to the relevant past as memory and to the future as hopes, plans, trepidations, and dreads. Mind wandering thus plays rapidly over loosely organized present, past, and future identity themes. As a universal human experience, mind wandering is spontaneous and not deliberate. In contrast to the spontaneity of mind wandering, freeing one's mind from a definable task in order to meditate or "free" associate is apt to be deliberate or prescribed.

Returning to diagram 5, let's say John's mind wanders to the examination he has taken that morning: "Did I get that third questions right? The stuff from another book could have been put in. Oh well, too late now. I've got to work on the paper for history, and I know that I've got some good ideas for that." All this happens in a spontaneous flash with a rapid shift of affect from anxious concern to reassurance and positive expectation. Or consider Kelly's after-date reflections: "I think he is really into me. We really lingered over that good-night kiss. I hope he isn't like Al – just setting me up for a hook-up and then bye-bye. Damn that hurt. . . . No. He's not like that. We really like doing stuff together."

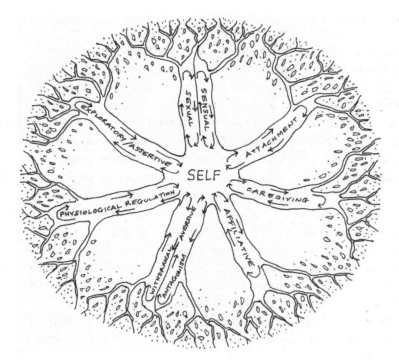

Diagram 4 The task-focused mind.

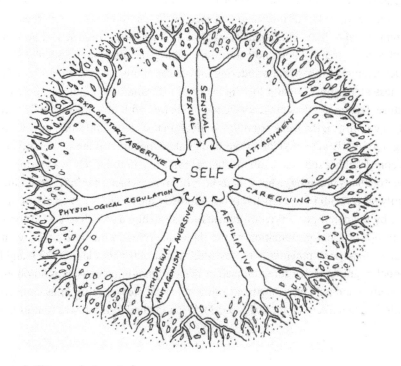

Diagram 5 The wandering mind.

140 Afterword

In the examples, John's mind ultimately wanders into the exploratory motivational system while Kelly starts with reflections drawn from her sensual-sexual motivational system, touches on a reassuring positive sensual experience, dips into a past aversive memory, and returns to an affirming attachment sharing. Our point is this: In mind wandering, the individual's mind taps into and lightly touches on the affects, intentions, and goals of one or more motivational systems. There is a flitting, fleeting reflection on lived experience in terms of evaluating the impact on one's sense of self. Present, past, and future scenes are contemplated perhaps ever so briefly in a way that reinforces both personal identity and intersubjective imagery and themes. Sometimes the contents of an individual's wandering mind may be situational and short-lived, while at other times the same images and themes will recur over and over. Diagram 5 accordingly places the primary focus on the sense of self in the center of multiavailable affects, intentions, and goals that characterize the motivational systems and that generate the wide range of human lived experiences and shifting intentions.

Along with its visual convenience as an illustration, this diagram points to two distinctions between the task-focused and wandering mind. The first has to do with the flow of information; the second has to do with fluctuating self-images. Informational flow from the foundational perceptual, cognitive, affective, memory, and recursive systems is continuous throughout life. In the task-focused diagrams we assume an intensity of informational flow sufficient to evoke an emergent affect, intention, and goal. The intensity of flow is, of course, modified in accordance with state changes – alert and calm; alert and in pain; alert and frightened, drowsy, asleep, and so forth. Mind wandering introduces another variable – a state of more or less alert calm – with a low intensity of informational input of a peremptory nature. Diagram 5 thus presents the top of the tree with little intense informational input coming up the trunk from the foundational systems and small arrows touching into lightly activated intentions and goals. A person driving on a familiar road in comfortably predictable circumstances finds his mind loosely wandering over a meeting he is planning, what friends he will invite, when a car in front of him suddenly slows with its red tail-lights on. Suddenly the driver is jerked out of his reverie by the peremptory flow of information signaling a switch to a focus on task.

In our original presentation of the three diagrams in our last book, we noted that each diagram potentially represented "constructs about identity that any individual might fantasize about himself or herself; imagining oneself as autonomous, as analyst and patient, as husband and wife, as mentor or pupil, or as caregiver or child" (Lichtenberg et al., 2011, p. 53). What we had in mind was that in fantasy and imagination identity is flexible and that each diagram portrayed a possible sense of being a subject or object in multiple identities of being a doer doing. We are now adding another source for the enlivenment of the sense of self through fluctuating self-images as illustrated by the rapid movement into and back of the various motivational branches in diagram 5. That is, today enlivening can also come through the momentary role of being a doer who is *not* engaged in a focused task but is off in a mind-cloud reflecting on his or her self-experience. These wanderings, the scientists tell us and both introspection and clinical observation readily confirm, are often reflections on the experience of some doing no matter whether in the past or future. Yet these fluctuating self-images also clearly have a potentially enlivening aspect. We have long felt that any metatheory, or any attempt at a metatheory, in psychoanalysis must take cognizance of the experiential self, motivational systems, foundational psychic capacities, and intersubjectivity. We have lately come to believe that such a metatheory must also include this newly formulated and still poorly explored dimension of the psyche, the wandering mind.

References

Adenzito, C., Adezatom, M., & Garbarini, F. (2006). The as if in cognitive science, neuroscience and anthropology. *Theory of Psychology, 16*, 747–759.

Arnetoli, C. (2002). Empathic networks: Symbolic representations in the Intersubjective Field. *Psychoanalytic Inquiry, 20*, 740–765.

Aron, L. (1996). *A meeting of minds*. Hillsdale, NJ: The Analytic Press.

Beebe, B., Jaffe, J., Markese, S., Buck, K., Chen, H., Cohen, P., . . . Feldstein, S. (2010). The origins of 12-month attachment: a microanalysis of 4-month mother-infant interaction. *Attachment and Human Development, 12*, 3–141.

Beebe, B., & Lachmann, F. M. (2002). *Infant research and adult treatment: Co-constructing interactions*. Hillsdale, NJ: The Analytic Press.

Belluck, P. (2013, October 3). For better social skills, scientists recommend a little Chekhov. *Mind*. Available at http://well.blogs.nytimes.com/2013/10/03/i-know-how-youre-feeling-i-read-chekhov/?_r=0

Benjamin, J. (1988). *The bonds of love: Psychoanalysis, feminism, and the problem of domination*. New York, NY: Pantheon Books.

Benjamin, J. (1995). *Like subjects, love objects*. New Haven, CT: Yale University Press.

Brandchaft, B. (1994). To free the spirit from its cell. In A. Goldberg (Ed.), *The widening scope of self psychology: Progress in self psychology* (Vol. 9, pp. 209–230). Hillsdale, NJ: The Analytic Press.

Brandschaft, B., Doctors, S., & Sorter, D. (2010). *Toward an emancipatory psychoanalysis*. New York: Routledge.

Brazelton, T. B. (1973, May). The neonatal behavioral assessment scale. The Brazelton Institute.

Brazelton, T. B. (1980, May 3). New knowledge about the infant from current research: Implications for psychoanalysis. Presented at a meeting of the American Psychoanalytic Association, San Francisco.

Brazelton, T. B. (1992, May). Touch and the fetus. Presented to the Touch Research Institute, Miami, FL.

Brooks, D. (2013, December 27). The Sidney Awards, part 1. *The New York Times*, p. A27.

Bucci, W. (1985). Dual coding: A cognitive model for psychoanalytic research. *Journal of the American Psychoanalytic Association, 33*, 571–607.

144 References

Bucci, W. (1997). *Psychoanalysis and cognitive science: A multiple code theory.* New York, NY: Guilford.

Bucci, W. (2002). The referential process, consciousness, and the sense of self. *Psychoanalytic Inquiry, 22,* 766–793.

Burlingham, D. (1949). The relation of twins to each other. *Psychoanalytic Study of the Child,* 3/4. 57–72.

Condon, P., Desbordes, G., Miller, W., & DeSteno, D. (2013). Meditation increases compassionate responses to suffering. *Psychological Science.* doi: 10.1177/0956797613485603

Damasio, A. (1994). *Descartes' error.* New York, NY: GP Putman's Sons.

Damasio, A. (1999). *The feeling of what happens.* New York, NY: Harcourt Brace.

DeCasper, A., & Fifer, W. (1980). Of human bonding: Newborns prefer their mothers' voices. *Science, 208,* 474–476.

DeCastro, F., Ayala, N., & Mayes, L. (2010). Maternal attributions of intentionality: Measuring adaptive and pathological internal projections. *JAPA, 58,* 545–556.

Edelman, G. (1987). *Neural Darwinism.* New York, NY: Basic Books.

Edelman, G. (1992). *Bright air, brilliant fire.* New York, NY: Basic Books.

Edelman, G. M. (1992). *Bright air, brilliant fire: On the matter of the mind.* New York, NY: Basic Books.

Eimas, P., Siqueland, W., Judezyk, P., & Vigerito, J. (1971). Speech perception in infants. *Science, 218,* 1138–1141.

Feinberg, T. (2009). *From axons to identity: Neurological explorations of the nature of the self.* New York, NY: Norton.

Fivaz-Depeursinge, E., & Corboz-Warnery, A. (1999). *The primary triangle.* New York, NY: Basic Behavioral Science.

Fonagy, P. (1991). Thinking about thinking: Some clinical and theoretical consideration in the treatment of a borderline patient. *International Journal of Psycho-Analysis, 72,* 639–656.

Fosshage, J. (1983). The psychological function of dreams: A revised psychoanalytic perspective. *Psychoanalysis and Contemporary Thought, 6*(4), 641–669. [Also in M. Lansky (Ed.). (1992). *Essential papers on dreams.* New York, NY: New York University Press.]

Fosshage, J. (1997a). Listening/experiencing perspectives and the quest for a facilitative responsiveness. In A. Goldberg (Ed.), *Conversations in self psychology: Progress in self psychology* (Vol. 13, pp. 33–55). Hillsdale, NJ: The Analytic Press.

Fosshage, J. (1997b). The organizing functions of dreams. *Contemporary Psychoanalysis, 33*(3), 429–458.

Fosshage, J. (1999). Different forms of intimacy: The case of Samantha. Presented at the 22nd Annual International Conference on the Psychology of the Self, Toronto, Ontario, Canada. (Unpublished manuscript).

Fosshage, J. (2000). The meanings of touch in psychoanalysis: A time for reassessment. *Psychoanalytic Inquiry, 20*(1), 21–43.

Fosshage, J. (2003). Contextualizing self psychology and relational psychoanalysis: Bidirectional influence and proposed syntheses. *Contemporary Psychoanalysis, 39*(3), 411–448.

Fosshage, J. (2005). The explicit and implicit domains in psychoanalytic change. *Psychoanalysis and Contemporary Thought, 6,* 641–669.

References 145

Fosshage, J. (2011). How do we "know" what we "know"? And change what we "know"? *Psychoanalytic Dialogues, 21*(1), 55–74.

Frank, R., & LaBarre, F. (2011). *The first year and the rest of our life: Movement, development, and psychotherapeutic change.* New York, NY: Routledge.

Freud, S. (1959). Symptoms inhibitions and anxiety. In *Standard edition* (Vol. 20, pp. 87–172). London: Hogarth Press. (Original work published 1926)

Freud, S. (1966). Project for a scientific psychology. In *Standard edition* (Vol. 1, pp. 283–392). London: Hogarth Press. (Original work published 1895)

Goleman, D. (2013). *Focus: The hidden driver of excellence.* New York, NY: Harper Collins.

Hamlin, J. K., Wynn, K., & Bloom, P. (2007). Social evaluation by preverbal infants. *Nature, 450,* 557–560.

Hamlin, J. K., Wynn, K., & Bloom, P. (2010). Three-month-olds show a negativity bias in their social interactions. *Developmental Science, 13*(6), 923–929.

Hamlin, J. K., Wynn, K., Bloom, P., & Mahajan, N. (2011). How infants and toddlers react to antisocial others. *Proceedings of the National Academy of Sciences, 108*(50), 19931–19936.

Harrison, A., & Tronick, E. (2011). "The noise monitor": A developmental perspective on verbal and non verbal meaning-making in psychoanalysis. *Journal of the American Psychoanalytic Assoicataion, 59,* 961–982.

Healy, M. (2010, August 30). An idle brain may be the self's workshop. *Los Angeles Times.*

Hoffman, J., Popbla, L., & Duhalde, C. (1998). Early stages of initiative and environmental response. *Infant Mental Health Journal, 19,* 355–377.

Jaffe, J., Beebe, B., Feldstein, S., Crown, C., & Jasnow, M. (2001). Rhythms of dialogue in early infancy. *Monographs of the Society for Research in Child Development, 66*(2, Serial No. 264), 1–132.

Knoblauch, S. (2000). *The musical edge of therapeutic dialogue.* Hillsdale, NJ: The Analytic Press.

Kohut, H. (1971). *The analysis of the self.* New York, NY: International Universities Press.

Kohut, H. (1977). *The Restoration of the Self.* New York, NY: International Universities Press.

Kohut, H. (1981). On empathy. In P. H. Ornstein (Ed.), *The search for the self: The selected writings of Heinz Kohut: 1978–1981* (Vol. 4, pp. 525–535). Madison, CT: International Universities Press.

Kuhl, P., & Meltzoff, A. (1982). The bimodal perception of speech in infancy. *Science, 218,* 1138–1141.

Lachmann, F. M. (2000). *Transforming aggression: Psychotherapy with the difficult-to-treat patient.* Northvale, NJ: Aronson.

Lachmann, F. M. (2008). *Transforming narcissism: Reflections of empathy, humor, and expectations.* New York, NY: The Analytic Press.

Lachmann, F. M. (2011).Perspectives on individuality: From cells to selves. In R. Frie & W. J. Coburn (Eds.), *Persons in context: The challenge of individuality in theory and practice* (pp. 107–118). New York, NY: Routledge.

Lane, R. (2008). Neural substrates of implicit and explicit emotional processes: A unifying framework for psychosomatic medicine. *Psychosomatic Medicine, 90,* 214–231.

Lehrer, J. (2007). *Proust was a neuroscientist.* Boston: Houghton Mifflin.

Lichtenberg, J. (1978). The testing of reality from the standpoint of the body self. *Journal of the American Psychoanalytic Association, 26,* 257–285.

Lichtenberg, J. (1989). *Psychoanalysis and motivation*. Hillsdale, NJ: Analytic Press.

Lichtenberg, J. (2005). Sanderian activation waves: A hypothesis of non-symbolic influence on moods. *Psychoanalytic Quarterly, 74*, 484–505.

Lichtenberg, J. (2008). *Sensuality and sexuality across the divide of shame*. New York, NY: The Analytic Press.

Lichtenberg, J., Lachmann, F., & Fosshage, J. (1989). *Psychoanalysis and motivation*. Hillsdale, NJ: The Analytic Press.

Lichtenberg, J., Lachmann, F., & Fosshage, J. (1996). *The clinical exchange: Technique from the standpoint of self and motivational systems*. Hillsdale, NJ: The Analytic Press.

Lichtenberg, J., Lachmann, F., & Fosshage, J. (2011). *Psychoanalysis and motivational systems: A new look*. New York, NY: Routledge

Litowitz, B. (2011). From dyad to dialogue: Language and the early relationship in American psychoanalytic theory. *Journal of the American Psychoanalytic Association, 59*, 483–508.

Llinas, R. (2001). *I of the vortex: From neurons to self*. Cambridge, MA: The MIT Press.

Lyon-Ruth, K. (2003). Dissociation and the parent-infant dialogue: Intersubjective dialogue, enactive representation, and the emergence of new forms of relational organization. *Psychoanalytic Dialogues, 19*, 576–617.

Mahler, M. (1968). *On human symbiosis and the vicissitudes of the individual*. New York, NY: International Universities Press.

Malatesta, C. & Haviland, J. (1983) In A. Editor and B. Editor (Eds.), *Relational psychoanalysis volume 2: Innovation and expansion*.

Mayes, L. C., & Cohen, D. J. (1996). Children's developing theory of mind. *Journal of the American Psychoanalytic Association, 44*, 117–142.

Meissner, W. (1968). Dreaming as process. *International Journal of Psychoanalysis, 49*, 63–79.

Miller, A. (1981). *Prisoners of childhood: The drama of the gifted child and the search for the true self*. New York, NY: Basic Books.

Miller, J. (1985). How Kohut actually worked. In A. Goldberg (Ed.), *Progress in self psychology* (Vol. 1, pp. 13–32). New York, NY: Guilford.

Modell, A. (2006). *Imagination and the meaningful brain*. Cambridge, MA: MIT Press.

Modell, A. (2009). Metaphor: The bridge between feelings and meaning. *Psychoanalytic Inquiry, 25*, 555–568.

Paivio, A. (1971). *Imagery and verbal processes*. New York, NY: Holt, Rinehart & Winston. (Reprinted in 1979, Hillsdale, NJ: Lawrence Erlbaum Associates.)

Paivio, A. (2007). *Mind and its evolution: A dual coding theoretical approach*. Mahwah, NJ: Erlbaum.

Panksepp, J. (1998). Affective: The Foundations of Human and Animal Emotions. New York: Oxford University Press.

Panksepp, J. (1998). The preconscious substitutes of consciousness: Affective states and the evolutionary origin of the self. *Journal of Consciousness Studies, 5*, 566–582.

Panksepp, J. (2008). The power of the word may reside in the power of affect. *Integrative Psychological and Behavioral Science, 42*, 47–55.

Piontelli, A. (1987). Infant observation from before birth. *International Journal of Psychoanalysis, 68*, 453–464.

Raichle, M., & Snyder, A. (2007). A default mode of brain function: A brief history of an evolving idea. *Neuroimage, 37*, 1083–1090.

References 147

Raichle, M. E., Macleod, A. M., Snyder, A. Z., Powers, W. J., Gusnard, D. A., & Shulman, G. L. (2001). A default mode of brain functioning. *Proceedings of the National Academy of Sciences, 96*(2), 676–682.

Rakoczy, H., & Schmidt, M. (2013). The early ontology of social norms. *Child Developmental Perspectives, 7*(1), 17–21.

Reik, T. (1949). *Listening with the third ear: The inner experience of a psychoanalyst.* New York, NY: Farrar, Straus and Company.

Reiser, M. (1990). *Memory in mind and brain.* New York, NY: Basic Books.

Rizzolatti, G., Fogassi, L., & Gallese, V. (2004). Cortical mechanisms subserving object grasping, action understanding, and imitation. In M. S. Gazzaniga (Ed.), *The new cognitive neurosciences* (3rd ed., pp. 427–440). Cambridge, MA: MIT Press.

Rovee-Collier, D., Sullivan, M., Ehright, M., Lucas, D., & Fagen, J. (1980). Reactivation of infant memory. *Science, 208*, 1159–1161.

Rumelhart, D., McClelland, J., & the PDP Research Group (Eds.). (1986). *Parallel distributed processing: Explorations in the microstructure of cognition.* Cambridge, MA: MIT Press.

Sander, L. (1983). To begin with: Reflections on ontogeny. In J. Lichtenberg & S. Kaplan (Eds.), *Reflections on self psychology* (pp. 85–104). Hillsdale, NJ: The Analytic Press.

Sander, L. W. (1977). The regulation of exchange in the infant-caretaker system and some aspects of the context-content relationship. In M. Lewis & L. Rosenbaum (Eds.), *Interaction, conversation, and the development of language* (pp. 133–156). New York, NY: Wiley.

Schooler, J. W., Smallwood, J., Christoff, K., Handy, T. C., Reichle, E. D., & Sayette, M. A. (2011). Meta-awareness, perceptual decoupling and the wandering mind. *Trends Cognitive Sciences, 15*, 319–326.

Shane, M., Shane, E., & Gales, M. (1998). *Intimate attachments: Toward a new self psychology.* New York, NY: Guilford Press.

Singer, F., & Fagen, J. (1992). Negative affect, emotional expression and forgetting in young infants. *Developmental Psychology, 28*, 48–57.

Slochower, J. (1996). *Holding and psychoanalysis: A relational perspective.* Hillsdale, NJ: The Analytic Press.

Smallwood, J., & Schooler, J. W. (2006). The restless mind. *Psychological Bulletin, 132*, 946–958.

Solano, L. (2010). Some thoughts between body and mind in the light of Wilma Bucci's multiple code theory. *International Journal of Psychoanalysis, 91*, 1445–1464.

Solomon, J., George, C., & DeJong, A. (1995). Children classified as controlling at age six: Evidence of disorganized representational strategies and aggression at home and at school. *Development and Psychopathology, 7*, 447–463.

Stern, D., Sander, L., Nahum, J., Harrison, A., Lyons-Ruth, K., Morgan, A., . . . Tronick, E. (1998). Non-interpretive mechanisms in psychoanalytic therapy: The "something more' than interpretation. *International Journal of Psycho-Analysis, 79*, 903–921.

Stern, D. B. (1997). Unformulated experience: From dissociation to imagination. In Hillsdale, NJ: The Analytic Press.

Stern, D. N. (1985). *The interpersonal world of the infant.* New York, NY: Basic Books.

Stolorow, R., & Atwood, G. (1992). *Contexts of being: The intersubjective foundation of psychological life.* Hillsdale, NJ: The Analytic Press.

148 References

Stuss, D. (1992). Biological and physiological development of executive function. *Brain and Cognition, 20*, 8–23.

Tolpin, M. (2002). Doing psychoanalysis of normal development: Forward edge transferences. *Progress in Self Psychology, 18*, 167–190.

Topel, E-M. (2004). Nonverbale interaktionen mit aggressiven Kinder und Jugendlichen [Nonverbal interactions with aggressive children and adolescents]. *Psychother. Soc., 6*, 145–167.

Topel, E-M., & Lachmann, F. M. (2007). Nonverbal dialogues orienting and looking behaviors between aggressive and violent children and adolescents and their therapist. *Journal of Infant, Child, and Adolescent, Psychotherapy, 6*, 285–307.

Tronick, E. (2002). A model of infant mood states and Sanderian affective waves. *Psychoanalytic Dialogues, 12*, 73–99.

Tronick, E., Als, J., Adamson, L., Wise, S., & Brazelton, T. (1978). The infant's response to entrapment between contradictory messages in face-to-face interaction. *Journal of the American Academy of Child & Adolescent Psychiatry, 17*, 1–13.

Tronick, E., & Cohn, J. (1989). Infant–mother face-to-face interaction: Age and gender differences in coordination and the occurrence of miscoordination. *Child Development 60*, 85–92.

Vivona, J. (2009). Embodied language in neuroscience and psychoanalysis. *Journal of the American Psychoanalytic Association 57*, 1327–1360.

Vouloumanos, A., & Welker, J. (2007). Listening to language at birth: Evidence for a bias for speech in neonates. *Developmental Science, 10*, 159–164.

Winnicott, D. (1941). The observation of infants in a set situation. *International Journal of Psychoanalysis, 22*, 229–249.

Winnicott, D. (1953). Transitional objects and transitional phenomena. In *Collected papers* (pp. 229–242). London: Tavistock, 1958.

Winnicott, D. W. (1965). *The maturational processes and the facilitating environment.* New York, NY: International Universities Press.

Woodhead, J. (2010). Trauma in the crucible of the parent-infant relationship: The baby's experience. In T. Bardon (Ed.), *Relational trauma in infancy*. London: Routledge.

Index

Page numbers in italic indicate figures and tables.

abuse 78, 79, 80, 83
affective activation waves 28–30, 59, 60, 69
affects and consciousness 25–8
Ainsworth's Strange Situation 54
Alan (case study) 115–21
Amazon woman 73, 74
animate objects 38
antisocial hinderer 18–20
anxiety 9, 30, 46, 55, 56, 96
attachment and affiliation 23, 24, 129
attention deficit disorder (ADD) 107, 115, 119
Attention Deficit Hyperactivity Disorder (ADHD) 107, 115, 119–25
attributions: in infancy 64–5; negative 33, 72; parental 75, 91
authentic self 73, 74, 91
aversion 18–20, 42–3, 125
aversive motivations 100, 102
aversiveness, infants and 25
avoidant attachment 53, 124
awe and admiration, experiences of 61–2

been there, done that experience 57
Behavior Modification treatments 96
being touched *see* self-touch and being touched
bidirectional mode 3, 33–5
biological clock 29, 60

boundary openness 136–7
Brazelton Neonatal Assessment Scale 53, 54

cancer, fear of 5, 6
caregiver-infant relationship 21, 49, 64, 66
caregiver touch 21, 22, 68
caregiving and loving, infants and 23, 25
case studies: Alan 115–21; Cora and Peggy 35–6; Edgar 101; Gianni and Guilia 15–16; Katie 11–13; Larry 92–6; Marco 121–6; Meg 113–14; Mrs. H 4–10; Roger 107–9; Samantha 72–92
Cat in the Hat, The 31, 48
children classified as controlling 44
cognition 58, 133, 134, 138
communications: case study 35–6; face-to-face 37; secure infants and 21; verbal 31, 34
comparator functions 18, 47, 48, 49
confidence and optimism, doer doing and 52–6
conflictivity 42
connectionist theory 59
consciousness: affects and 25–8; core 26, 27, 44, 48; primary 12, 14, 27, 28
controlling children 44
cooperation: failure in 43–4; by infant and caregiver 40–3, 68–9
coping skills 54–5
core consciousness 26, 27, 44, 48

daydreaming 102, 103, 107, 119, 121
default mode network 105, 106, 107
depression 30, 33, 63, 101, 117
developmental processes 1, 71–2, 92, 97
disciplined spontaneous engagement 114
disorganized infants 22
disruption-repair sequence 52, 55, 64
disruptions 35, 69, 72, 76, 80, 85
distress state, infants and 21, 25, 36,
 54–5, 64
doer doing: affects and consciousness
 and 25–8; confidence and optimism
 and 52–6; in a dyadic interchange *135*;
 initiatives and cooperation and 40–3;
 insecurity and pessimism and 52–6;
 Katie case study 11; lived experience
 and 2; mind of *132*; Mrs. H case study
 4, 5, 11, 13; nonhuman environment
 and 38–40; prenatal predispositions
 and 15–16; social competence
 and 36–8; *see also* memory; mind
 wandering; sense of self
dreams: inner experience and 75, 77;
 memory and 80–1
dyadic system 21–3

early development 1, 4, 6–7, 10, 20, 61
early memory 56–62
Edgar (case study) 101
emotional schemas 45, 46
empathic listening 74, 100, 101, 102, 113,
 114
empathy: capacity for 66; fiction reading
 and 111–13
enlivening experience, sharing moments of
 84, 86, 87, 88, 91
exploration, infants and 24, 58, 95
exploratory system 45, 46, 137

false self 34, 65
fiction reading, empathy and 111–13
focused attention 101, 102
foundational systems 58, 133, 134, 140
free association 109–10

Gianni and Guilia (case study) 15–16
Gone Girl (Flynn) 111
group therapy 85, 91

helper-hinderer scenes 18–19
humor 67, 89, 92, 94, 96
hyperactivity 44, 119, 120

idling brain 106
imagistic symbolic processing: description
 of 14; early memory and 56–62; inner
 experience and 75; of lived experience
 16–18; in prenatal period 15; preverbal
 infants and 23; sense of self and 13–14
implicit memory 14, 16, 31, 57–60
inanimate objects 19, 38, 40, 128
infancy: attributions in 64–5; introduction
 to 1–2; lived experience and 16–30;
 motivational systems in 23–5;
 processing experience and 13; sense of
 self and 2–4, 11–16
infant-caregiver interplay 33–4, 38, 53
infants: assessing stress in 53–5;
 developmental origins of capacity of
 18; disorganized 22; early development
 and 61; initiatives by 40–3; loving
 and caregiving and 23, 25; nonhuman
 environment and 38–40; self-regulation
 by 53; social competence of 36–8; speech
 development by 31–3; subsymbolic and
 imagistic symbolic processing in 14;
 see also doer doing
informational flow 140
initiatives/initiation: disruption of 43–4;
 by infants 40–3; predicting patterns of
 65–6
inner integral self 73, 91
insecure attachment 37, 54, 55
insecurity and pessimism, doer doing and
 52–6
intense conflict 42, 76
interactive regulation 36, 40, 93, 118, 125
intersubjective relations 1, 86, 101
intimate relationships 118, 137

"junk genes" 106

Katie (case study) 11–13, 17

Larry (case study) 92–6
literary fiction reading 112–13
lived experiences: of abuse 83; affective
    moments of 96; building conceptual
    map of 13; doer doing and 2; early
    memory and 58; imagistic aspect of
    16–18; infancy and 16–30; introduction
    to 1; of Katie and other infants 17;
    mental state disruptions and 52–3;
    qualities and experiences for 69–70; of
    self-touch and being touched 21–3, 68;
    sharing moments of 67; trends emergent
    in 63–70
loving and caregiving, infants and 23, 25

Marco (case study) 121–6
match-mismatch-match experiences 54, 55
match-mismatch-rematch patterns 53
maternal responses 42
meditation 110–11
Meg (case study) 113–14
memory: dreams and 80–1; Edelman's
    view on 27; implicit 14, 16, 31, 57–60;
    procedural 46, 69; subsymbolic and
    imagistic processing and 56–62;
    traumatic and painful 81–2; unconscious
    and conscious 51
mental functioning 131, 133
mental processing, sense of an agentic self
    and 44–62
metacognition 103, 104
metaphoric processes 13, 50, 51, 52, 93,
    134
metaphoric touch 68, 69
midrange coordination 53, 54
mind wandering: conclusion about 126–9;
    as a default mode network 105, 106,
    107; defined 103; fiction reading and
    111–13; free association and 109–10;
    gone awry 114–26; imaginative analyst

and 113–14; introduction to 99–100; key
    functions related to 104; meditation and
    110–11; mind at task and 100–2, 107–9,
    138, 140; neural networks and 105, 106;
    portrayal of 138, *139*; processes related
    to 103; sense of self and 103–7; short-
    lived 140; *Ulysses* example and 102
mood activation 22, 28–30, 63–4
mother-baby interplay 56, 59
mother-infant dyadic 21, 35
motivational systems: comparator functions
    and 18; conclusion about 128; diagrams
    related to 131–41; emergence of 23–5;
    exploratory/assertive 57; interaction of
    134, 136; prenatal period and 15; sense
    of self and 45–50, 96–7; sensual/sexual
    21, 140; tree limbs representing *132*,
    133, 134; types of 100
motor activities 17, 18, 39, 46, 127
Mrs. H (case study) 4–10
multiple code theory 45–6
musical affective prosody 32

narrative capacity 18–20, 66
narratives: forming and sharing 66;
    Samantha case study 75, 76
negative affects 22, 29, 57–9, 63–4, 77
negative attributions 33, 72
negative behaviors 18, 19
negative experiences 28, 29, 59, 85
negative mood 28, 29, 30, 59
neonates: prenatal predispositions' influence
    on 15–16; processes related to 2; sense of
    self and 11–14
neural maps 27, 47
neural networks: mind wandering and 105,
    106; nonhuman environment and 38, 39;
    perfectionist expectations and 90; sense
    of an agentic self and 2; subsymbolic
    processing and 14
neural processes 2, 105
nonconscious affects 26, 27
nonconscious processing 48, 129
nonhuman environment 38, 39

Index

open mouth experience 9, 56
openness of boundaries 136–7
optimism and confidence, doer doing and 52–6

panic attacks 94, 96
parallel speech 122
perceptual decoupling 103, 104
perfectionism 90, 91
pessimism and insecurity 52–6
physical touch 68, 87
physiological regulation 23, 102, 125
playful interaction 67–8
popular fiction reading 112–13
positive or negative mood activation 22, 28–30, 63–4
pregnancy, fear of 5, 6
prenatal predispositions 15–16
primary consciousness 12, 14, 27, 28
procedural memory 46, 69
procrastination 115, 116, 126
proto-self-experience 12, 15–16, 26–7, 30–1, 47–9
Psychoanalysis and Motivational Systems: A New Look (Lichtenberg et al.) 100, 131

reflective processing 77, 80, 85
REM sleep 13, 14
resilience 10, 53, 63
Rip Van Winkle story 87, 88
Roger (case study) 107–9
rough-and-tumble play 120, 121, 123, 124, 126
Round House, The (Erdrich) 111

Samantha (case study) 72–92
secure attachment 21, 33, 37, 54
self-confidence 24, 37, 56
self-experience 24, 26, 112, 117, 141
self-expression 56, 127
self-images 140, 141
self-object relationship 74, 80, 84
self-regulation 22, 36, 37, 91, 93, 125

self-sensual arousal 25
self-touch and being touched 21–3, 68, 69
self-worth 12, 108
sense of an agentic self: development of 1–4; implicit memory and 60; mental processing and 44–62; motivational systems and 45–50; Mrs. H case study 4–10; reflections on the origin of 62–70; verbal symbol system and 50–2
sense of authenticity 65
sense of being known 65, 66, 87, 89
sense of betrayal 78, 79, 80
sense of self: attachment and affiliation and 24; building confident 56; conclusion about 128–9; developmental processes and 1, 71, 72, 92, 97; emergence of 3–4, 11–13; empathic listening and 114; imagistic symbolic processing and 13–14; infancy and 2–4, 11–16; initiatives and cooperation and 40–3; introduction to 1; motivational systems and 96–7; neonates and 11–14; with others 30–44; subsymbolic processing and 13–15; *see also* mind wandering
sensory experience 48, 60
sensory modalities 14, 16, 46
sexual fantasies 116, 126
sexual feelings 78, 79, 89, 115
silence 5–9, 113
Sins of the Mother (Steel) 111
social competence 36–8
social helper 18–20
social interactions 36
social norms 20, 66–7, 69, 72, 86, 95
speech elements, development of 31–3
spirit of playfulness, generating 67–8
still-face assessment 54, 55
Strange Situation assessment 54, 55
stress, tests for assessing 53–5
subsymbolic processing: early memory and 56–62; motivational systems and 46–7; neural networks and 14;

nonhuman environment and 39; sense of self and 13–15

surprise, awe, and admiration, experiencing moments of 69–70

symbolic systems 50, 51

Symptoms, Inhibitions and Anxiety (Freud) 15

task-focused learning and mind 117, *139*, 140

therapeutic experiences 4, 20, 95

therapeutic relationship 38, 61, 64, 70, 114

therapy: experiences of cooperation and 68; group 85, 91; lived experiences and 63–70; reflections about 96–7; sense of being and 66

traumatic losses 77

Tronick's still-face situation 54

Ulysses (Joyce) 102

verbal and prosody patterns 32–3

verbal symbolic processing 39, 46–52, 64, 133

victimization, sense of 79

wandering mind *see* mind wandering

wave theory 28, 30, 59

yawning symptom 8

zoning out 106, 107

eBooks
from Taylor & Francis

Helping you to choose the right eBooks for your Library

Add to your library's digital collection today with Taylor & Francis eBooks. We have over 50,000 eBooks in the Humanities, Social Sciences, Behavioural Sciences, Built Environment and Law, from leading imprints, including Routledge, Focal Press and Psychology Press.

Choose from a range of subject packages or create your own!

Benefits for you
- Free MARC records
- COUNTER-compliant usage statistics
- Flexible purchase and pricing options
- All titles DRM-free.

Benefits for your user
- Off-site, anytime access via Athens or referring URL
- Print or copy pages or chapters
- Full content search
- Bookmark, highlight and annotate text
- Access to thousands of pages of quality research at the click of a button.

Free Trials Available
We offer free trials to qualifying academic, corporate and government customers.

eCollections

Choose from over 30 subject eCollections, including:

Archaeology	Language Learning
Architecture	Law
Asian Studies	Literature
Business & Management	Media & Communication
Classical Studies	Middle East Studies
Construction	Music
Creative & Media Arts	Philosophy
Criminology & Criminal Justice	Planning
Economics	Politics
Education	Psychology & Mental Health
Energy	Religion
Engineering	Security
English Language & Linguistics	Social Work
Environment & Sustainability	Sociology
Geography	Sport
Health Studies	Theatre & Performance
History	Tourism, Hospitality & Events

For more information, pricing enquiries or to order a free trial, please contact your local sales team:
www.tandfebooks.com/page/sales

www.tandfebooks.com